P9-DCU-487

'Round the world cooking library
American Cooking

A sharing of the fresh abundance of the good earth

**Written by
Irena Kirshman**

international
authority on
American cooking

'Round the World Books Inc. • New York • Toronto

Contents

Written by	Irena Kirshman, graduate Cordon Bleu Cooking School, lecturer on international cuisines, food consultant
Editor and contributor	Susan Wright
Associate editor	Gladys McConnell
Cover and recipe photos	Irwin Horowitz, New York City
Additional introduction photos	see credit list on page 100
Design and drawings	Rosemarijn van Limburg Stirum, Amsterdam
Created by	Meijer Pers B.V., Amsterdam, The Netherlands
Typeset by	Internationaal Zetcentrum B.V., Wormerveer, The Netherlands
Printed by	Drukkerij Meijer B.V., Wormerveer, The Netherlands
Bound by	Proost en Brandt N.V., Amsterdam, The Netherlands
Publisher and World Distributor	'Round the World Books Inc., New York, Toronto

All rights reserved.
No part of this book may be reproduced in any form, by mimeography or any other means, without permission in writing.

Copyright © 1973, 1974 by Meijer Pers B.V., Amsterdam, The Netherlands

Cup measures in this book are based on an eight ounce cup.

America at the table

In the beginning, the cooking of every country was a reflection of its own geography. It was the sun and the rain, the mountains and the valleys which alone determined whether the first people would eat meat or fish, fruit or nuts, truffles or bird's nest soup. Earnest prayers to ancient gods and tribal fertility ceremonies may have helped to bring a greater abundance of food, but except for the gift of manna, neither magic nor religious beliefs increased the variety.

Gradually man, spurred on by necessity and his own ingenuity, learned to make the best of whatever was available. Chinese emperors dined philosophically at a table set with a hundred exquisite morsels, balancing their dishes with harmonious respect. In Egypt, magnificently intricate golden serving vessels graced the tables of kings fourteen centuries before Christ was born. Wealthy Romans gorged themselves on stuffed boar, meat puddings, herbed lobsters and marinated chops. They ate wild birds and omelettes and drank an infinite variety of wines. And while the Holy Roman Empire was crumbling in an orgy of gluttony, Frenchmen were slowly and carefully maturing their cheeses in the caves of Roquefort.

But though the privileged and powerful may have eaten well, the poor people were hungry.

Under banners of religion, king, country or just plain hunger, armies have roved across greener pastures since the beginning of time. These invading foreign forces changed the food not only of their own country, but of every culture they encountered. They bought or stole or traded seeds, salt, spices, domesticated animals and new ideas. Italians learned about spaghetti and noodles from Marco Polo's travels to the court of the Kubla Khan, or maybe it was the other way around. Mohammed sold spices to feed his mystical armies as they journeyed from the east to the west. Salt was traded between the Aegean and southern Russia, and tea that grew in China, Ceylon and India was brewed in England.

All this time America was standing alone, isolated and unexplored. There was practically no contact between its native Indian population and the civilizations of the rest of the world. The American Indians cultivated corn, peas, beans, pumpkins, watermelons and sunflowers. They ate the sweet potatoes and roots which were growing wild and hunted for their meat with simple weapons. They did not domesticate any animals. Milk was made from corn or ground nuts. There was no butter or cheese. The food was cooked simply and easily by boiling or roasting over an open fire. The contrast between the

A herd of Hereford cattle graze on the fertile land under the watchful eyes of the cowboys.

The mechanization of huge farms has resulted in fast, efficient and economical harvesting of wheat in the flat plains of the middle west.

Indian food and that of most of the rest of the world was that of a primitive culture compared with the civilization of centuries. Imagine then the plight of the Pilgrims. When the first settlers came to America at the beginning of the seventeenth century, they arrived weary, ill, hungry and exhausted. There was nothing for them to eat and nowhere for them to sleep. There were no markets or trading posts for them to buy those things which they considered the basic necessities of life. For the most part, the Pilgrims were thinkers, not workers, and had no knowledge of hunting, fishing or cultivating the land. In fact, their new lives had almost nothing in common with their previous experiences, and it is not surprising that four out of every five of the original founders of Jamestown died of starvation within the first year. The one hundred and two Pilgrims who arrived in Provincetown a few years later fared somewhat better. They survived on lobsters, oysters, clams and fish and, because they brought seeds, domesticated animals and a few farming tools with them, they were slightly more prepared to face their new surroundings. They immediately started building shelters for themselves and began to clear the ground for planting. Yet without the help of the Indians, many would have suffered the same fate as the early

Jamestown pioneers.
The Indians had a lasting effect on American cooking. They taught the Pilgrims how to plant their crops and cook the fruit of their labors. Gradually the Pilgrims adapted these 'foreign' ingredients into new combinations to suit their own needs and the foundation of a new style of cooking was laid. These early 'American' recipes were written in a blank book. Unlike all other countries, there was no established culinary heritage. There was not even a kitchen.

From the earliest times, the food was prepared as quickly and as simply as possible. Elegance in the preparation was not only impossible to achieve but would have been frowned on as being frivolous by the stern, hard working Puritans who had to struggle to produce any food at all.

It is interesting to see how the patterns and values established by the early settlers have persisted until the present time, and understandable that a large quantity of food continues to be regarded as a blessing. A magnificent steak cooked over a modern version of the old Indian fire is a symbol both of security and achievement, and the simplicity of the preparation is in keeping with the early American ethic. Yet, though these traditions of American cooking remain, the contrast between the food of the

colonists and the present day is astounding.
The bounty of America is seemingly limitless, for there is hardly a food which cannot be found somewhere in this vast fertile land.
The climate of America ranges from semi-Arctic to semi-tropical, from desert to lush grazing ground and from hills and plains to fertile valleys. Americans hunt wild game from icy Alaska to the mountain states of Colorado, Wyoming and Idaho and on through Texas and the south. Hundreds of varieties of fish swim the salt and fresh waters. Vegetables and fruits cross the boundaries of the states and the seasons. There is enough wine to cheer the nation and sufficient wheat to feed not only two hundred million Americans, but other countries too.
The gifts that Nature provided have been coaxed, crossbred and cross-fertilized into new hardy combinations by Luther Burbank and the agricultural researchers, and the ready acceptance of new machinery and new methods of farming have resulted in even greater yields from the land. Trucks careen through the night over unending miles of rails and roads, crisscrossing the nation to deliver the bounty. Long Island ducks are roasted in Oregon, pineapples from Hawaii are dusted with sugar in Nevada, New England sends her

lobsters to Oklahoma and Florida's oranges arrive for breakfast in New York.

Not only does the food travel across the country, but the people themselves are still constantly moving from state to state in search of a better life. It is now becoming more and more difficult to define regional boundaries and differences in the style of cooking from one section to another. Certainly some places still retain their own specialties, sometimes because particular foods are more plentiful and so more economical in one area than another, and sometimes as a result of the influence of immigrants who settled long enough to establish the foods of their own culture.

Some of the typical foods of New England are easily traced to the time of the early settlers, and surely the Indians must have had a hand in the first clam bake. Lobster and clams have now become synonymous with New England, though in pre-pollutionary times the Hudson river teemed with so many lobsters that they were considered too simple to set before a guest. Many of the recipes for boiled lobster, steamed clams, fish chowder, codfish cheeks and salt codfish balls have survived almost unchanged to the present time. The New England boiled dinner was first made in an iron pot

suspended over an open fire. This pot would often be one of the only cooking utensils owned by a family. The corned beef was simmered for several hours and other vegetables were added when the beef was almost tender. The virtue of this dish then, as now, lay not only in its delicious flavor, but in its method of cooking. It required little attention; leftovers were the added bonus for another day and could be made easily into red flannel hash with the addition of diced cooked beets. Pork was the first meat to be eaten in early colonial times. Pigs are such agreeable animals and so easily contented. The first New England pigs foraged in the woods and fed on wild nuts until they were plump enough to become pork, ham and bacon. The bacon pieces found their way into the clam chowder and the pork was salted to preserve it for the winter. The colonists taught themselves how to bake the Indian beans, flavoring them with salt pork and a touch of molasses or maple syrup for sweetness. Brown bread was the accompaniment to the baked beans because rye was plentiful and wheat was difficult to grow in so cold a climate.

Some people have said that one of the most distinctive characteristics of American cooking is its quality of sweetness. The first American foods were sweetened with

honey and maple syrup rather than sugar, and the fondness for sweet foods is a unique and distinctive aspect of American cooking not only in New England but throughout the country. Sweet breads are served for breakfast, powdered sugar is dusted on the French toast and pancakes, and waffles are unthinkable without the addition of maple or corn syrup. Sticky honey buns and pecan rolls, banana breads and other sweet breads are served for dinner, and fruit salads molded with gelatin appear regularly with both meat and poultry. Sweet wines are often preferred to dry wines, and the country flows with sodas and colas. Ice cream is made into enough flavors to stagger the imagination and then sweetened with chocolate, caramel and hot fudge sauce. The cakes are large and sweet and cotton candy delights every child.

In fact, much of America's history is associated with sugar. The cane was brought to the West Indies by Columbus and though the industrious planters all withered and died, the sugar cane flourished as it had never done before. Later, large plantations were established in the southern states and almost two thirds of the slaves brought to America worked in the cane fields until the time of the civil war. Lousiana discovered an economical way to refine the cane into sugar and by the turn

of the eighteenth century it was, for a brief time, selling a quarter of all the world's exportable sugar. New York later became, and still is, the sugar trading capital of the world.

America did not remain in isolation for long. New Englanders were not content to live on a diet of fish and beans. Soon the fishing and whaling boats were built sturdily enough to navigate the seas and trade in spices. Merchant schooners sailed from every harbor along the coast of New England, enduring voyages of great hardship lasting two or three years, to bring back their precious cargo. For a while, the spice fleet was protected by such government ships as the Columbia, the Constitution and the Potomac.

The profit from the spice trade was immense and America's first millionaire, Elias Derby, made his fortune from pepper. At the beginning of the nineteenth century, the tiny seaport of Salem was paying five percent of the expenses of the federal government from import duties levied on pepper alone. The bulk of this cargo was exported to Europe and new trade links were rapidly established. The remaining spices were sold throughout the colonies and became an indispensable part of American cooking.

The tale is told of certain unscrupulous Yankee traders

who whittled small pieces of wood to resemble nutmegs and then sold them to unsuspecting Connecticut housewives. The good women were so delighted with the price of the 'nutmegs,' they bought them eagerly, only to discover the deception too late. The nutmeg is now part of the state flag of Connecticut and serves as warning for its citizens to be constantly watchful and alert.

Large cities such as New York, San Francisco and New Orleans have contributed complete dishes rather than natural ingredients to the rest of the country. Lobster Newburg, Vichyssoise and the Waldorf Salad all originated in New York. Caesar Salad was created in San Francisco, and the chefs of New Orleans combined French, Southern and African foods into an entirely new group of distinctive dishes.
Many of America's most loved dishes originated in other countries, and spaghetti with meat balls, borscht, pizza and beef Stroganoff are now as American as apple pie (which was first made in England). The cities focus the effect that immigration has had on American cooking. When the new arrivals remained in one neighborhood, they recreated the dishes of their original country first in their homes, then in the ingredients to be found in their shops and

ultimately in their restaurants. A market was created for foods from all over the world. In New York it is possible to buy rice from Italy, Persia and India. There is dried tamarind rind, date nectar and Hungarian paprika. Bread comes daily from France and cakes are flown in from Vienna. There is smoked breast of German goose and cheese made from Greek ewe's milk. These rare and exotic ingredients reflect only the surface of the wide variety of foods which are prepared in homes across the country.

Though large areas of the middle Atlantic states of New York, New Jersey, Pennsylvania, Delaware and Maryland are highly industrialized, the remaining land is rich farming country. New Jersey, the garden state, supplies New Yorkers and the neighboring states with much of its fresh produce. The Pennsylvania Dutch people, who are not Dutch at all but of German descent, live in the heart of the lush dairy farming region of Pennsylvania. They make up a completely separate self-sufficient community which neither affects nor is affected by the rest of America. They choose to live by themselves and cook solid, plain, substantial food and make marvelous pickles and preserves. They have the distinction of being the only clearly identifiable regional cooks of America.

All of America is united in its love of hamburgers and milk shakes.

Though most food in America is bought in supermarkets, many cities also have smaller fruit and vegetable markets where the fresh produce is displayed like precious jewels. In the country, farmers truck the fruits of their own land to the market place.

Like the New Englanders, the people of the middle Atlantic states have a wide variety of fish from which to choose. There are the littleneck and cherrystone clams and a wealth of fish all along the coast, spilling into a treasure trove of marine life in Chesapeake Bay. An old city market in Baltimore claims to offer over a hundred varieties of fish for sale in a year. These all arrive in their appointed season and range from oysters and terrapins to spring shad and the famous Maryland crabs.
The crab feasts of Maryland are duplicated in other parts of the country too, and their characteristics are similar everywhere. Each diner is equipped with a crab hammer and the table is spread with newspapers to await the arrival of the crabs. They come scarlet and steaming, boiled with spices so hot that they slash their burning fire across the tongue of the novice who doesn't know whether to gasp for air or take a gulp of beer.

Though part of the South was among the original thirteen colonies, the food of this region is quite different from other parts of the country. The South has been less influenced by foreign immigration than by its own traditions of slavery and the long lingering effects of the economic disaster of the post-Civil War period. Pork and chicken, both inexpensive foods,

are popular in the South and are cooked in distinctive ways. Country ham and red eye gravy, chitterlings and collard green are southern specialties. Vegetables are simmered for hours with salt pork and fat back. Flour is milled to a softer texture to be baked into quick breads and biscuits. Southerners are fond of grits for breakfast, and deep fried foods such as Southern fried chicken, batter fried fish, hush puppies and French fries for lunch and dinner. With the exception of the larger cities like Atlanta and New Orleans, there are fewer fine restaurants in the South than in the North and the West. Florida, warmed by the Gulf Stream, basks in year round sunshine and is a tourist paradise as well as a home for many retired people from all over America. It is a state of date and coconut palms, of oranges, lemons and limes, of stonecrabs, pompano and shrimp. Travel is an integral part of Florida and her plentiful supply of shrimp is a gift from a mother shrimp who takes her annual vacation away from her home in Florida and journeys to the dry Tortugas. She descends to a depth of a hundred and twenty feet and leaves half a million babies, in the form of larvae, to fend for themselves and promptly returns to the sunshine state. The larvae drift towards the shore developing five legs on their heads, ten on

their bodies and, to balance things nicely, five sections to the tail. This symmetrical equipment enables them to make sudden dives, either backwards or forwards, to escape other sea-going travelers who have a fondness for baby shrimp. If they are not caught in a backward dive by an open-mouthed predator, they are netted by the shrimp boats. They are hauled aboard, frozen and dropped neatly, with preservatives added, into a printed transparent plastic bag for sale in supermarkets all over America.

The shrimp comes in all sorts of colors from the raw 'green' variety, which have a slightly green border around the edge of their tails, to gray, pink and brown. New varieties are constantly being discovered at deeper and deeper depths to satisfy the insatiable national appetite. They arrive on the table in many sizes and their value is calculated according to how many can dance on the head of a pin. Others are so large that eight shrimp will weigh a pound.

Florida is a state of hotels and hotel cooking and French, Italian and Cuban cooks have created many fine restaurants though, like the South and much of America, the best food is found in the homes.

Louisiana is the birthplace of Creole cooking. The state was Indian territory before it was

ruled by the Spanish and settled by French, English and American travelers from other states. The plantations were worked by African slaves, and from this varied group of people, a particular style of cooking was developed. Creole cooking is characterized by its most famous dish, the gumbo, which is a cross between a thick soup and a thin stew. It can be made from shrimp or shellfish, chicken or game which is simmered in a hearty broth with tomatoes, green pepper, thyme, bay leaf, filé powder ground from sassafras, rice, beans and okra, until it emerges rich and fragrant and mouthwateringly delicious. Some gumbos omit the okra, though it is this African word for the vegetable which gives the dish its name.

Texas and the southwest states of New Mexico and Arizona are cattle country and it is said that cowboys drove over ten million head of cattle to the market in the twenty years between 1870 and 1890. The rugged cowboys themselves created a culture of romance which has contributed to the eating habits of Americans. They brought to the country as a whole not only their love of beef, but a renewed dedication to outdoor cooking. Without the cowboys it hardly seems possible that Hollywood and television would have survived to spawn that other American phenomenon, the vast

industry devoted to snack foods. (The Indians thought of popcorn!) Continuous eating seems to have a calming effect on the stomach and mind as the suspense of cowboy and Indian adventures unfold to the final crunch.

Texas is the home of the barbeque and a style of eating known as Tex-Mex, which is a combination of Indian and Texas cowboy cooking. Enchiladas, frijoles and tortillas are common in Texas, though it was a German who discovered how to extract the pulp from the chilis and then created chile con carne. Many of the Tex-Mex dishes are the heritage from the Spanish settlers who lived and established missions not only in the southwest but also in California and the far west. The Spanish influence has been immense throughout this region for they brought cattle, pigs and chickens to America and planted oranges, lemons, olives and the grapes which were the beginning of the vast vineyards and wineries of California. The Texas cattle were eventually fattened on the corn of the Midwest before traveling on to the stockyards of Chicago. There the methods of cooking beef were Polish rather than Spanish. As the Poles settled in Illinois, the Dutch came to Michigan, and Iowa became the home of immigrants from Czechoslovakia. Each nationality left its mark on the cooking of the region. Sauerbraten became as familiar in the Midwest as the boiled beef dinner of New England. New food ideas from the Midwest were fast to spread across the country. Hot dogs and ice cream were both sold for the first time in St. Louis, and it is said that the first American hamburgers also came from the Midwest. The word 'hamburger' has a loose connection with the German town of Hamburg. The city once traded extensively with Russia where tartar steak was a favorite food. The people of Hamburg cooked the raw ground beef and the name of the dish became 'hamburger.' Americans served the hamburger in a bun so that the hungry nation would not burn its fingers. The German people of Wisconsin make as many varieties of sausage as there are flavors of ice cream. And when the sausages are served there is always plenty of German beer to be drunk. In fact, there is enough beer from Milwaukee to sustain several stadiums of sports fans.

The importance of the Midwest has been largely underestimated in the role it has played in American cooking. For how could America be America without hot dogs, hamburgers, beer and ice cream?

Peanut butter was also an idea from St. Louis. Two hundred and forty thousand tons of peanut butter will become a reality this year. (To calculate the number of peanut butter and jelly sandwiches consumed in America would cause a computer to jam.)

Just as St. Louis provided a lunch of peanut butter sandwiches, so Battle Creek in Michigan brought packaged breakfast foods to America. Here Dr. Graham in the 1830's expounded his theories of nutrition and graham flour to his disciples. So impressive were the discussions that Mr. Post, a patient in the sanitarium which was established by Dr. Graham's followers, went into the cereal business himself and created Postum and 'Elija's Manna,' a name which was later modified to Grape Nuts. Dr. Harvey Kellogg became the director of the sanitarium and innovated a new breakfast idea. Being a kind man, he tried to think of something to give to a patient who had broken his teeth on a piece of zwieback and inadvertently invented cornflakes. The dairy farms of Wisconsin provided the milk to pour over the cornflakes and yet another phase in American eating was launched.

The plains states of the Dakotas, Nebraska, Kansas and Oklahoma are known as the bread basket of America. Here, mile upon mile of wheat for the bread is sown, harvested and milled for Americans all over the country. American bread is one of the strangest paradoxes of American food, for in spite of the unlimited abundance of wheat, technology has concentrated less on the esthetic goodness of a crusty loaf of bread than on the problems of transporting flour so that it will not spoil. The wheat germ, the very heart of the flour, is extracted and fed to the cattle. When the wheat germ is removed, the shelf life of the flour is extended considerably, but without its heart. Commercial American bread is left also without a soul. The only good bread to be found in America is that which is baked at home or in small neighborhood bakeries. This is somewhat surprising because there has been a traditional respect for good bread in America.

The cowboy cook was an expert at making sourdough bread and biscuits. He maintained a pot of sourdough starter and its vitality was his first concern at all times. Each day, he mixed the correct proportions of flour and water into the sourdough starter and set it out in the sun to ferment. A little of the fermented dough was returned to the pot for the next day and the remainder was baked into bread. At night, the precious pot of starter was wrapped in a blanket to keep it warm, and if it was a cold night, the cook took it to bed with him. It was more than his life was worth to let the yeast freeze and become worthless. Sourdough bread sustained the gold prospectors on their arduous treks to the far west and it is still a popular bread there.

In the mountain states, the hunting season brings wild game to the tables and icy waters yield an abundance and variety of fish from the trout and salmon of Oregon to Olympia oysters from the state of Washington. The berries, orchard fruits and vegetables are as sweet and delicately flavored as any in the world.

The fertile valleys of California have perhaps the richest harvest of all. Fruit and vegetables are abundant in every season of the year and are grown in sufficient quantity to supply the needs of the nation. Not only does California have more produce and more people than any other state, it also has more grapes, and the quality of the California wines improves each year.

Grapes, grown and ripened in almost continuous sunshine, are gathered for winemaking in both New York State and California.

The entire history of the wines of America, like its food, is different from that of other countries. The vineyards of Europe are almost all planted in soil which is too poor to support other forms of cultivation, yet in California, which produces three quarters of the American wines, the vines nestle in lush green valleys exposed to almost continuous predictable sunshine. The Jesuit missionaries traveling north from Mexico planted the first grapes in California. These were named 'mission' grapes as nobody knew their varietal name. The plantings were begun in the late 1700's and the small amount of wine which remained from the religious observances for which they were intended was drunk locally. No attempt was made to experiment with the grape varieties at that time nor to discover which vine would produce the best wine in a particular location. The grapes, like Topsy, just grew until the missions were abandoned.

At the beginning of the eighteenth century, a Hungarian named Count Heraszthy began to change everything and almost singlehandedly put California on the way to becoming a wine-producing state. At the request of the state government, he planted literally thousands of different vines from cuttings he had gathered in Europe. Count Herazthy was followed by a group of dedicated men from Czechoslovakia, France, Italy and Prussia who established the great vineyards which are still thriving today.

The growth of the wines of California follows the pattern in which much of the cooking in America has developed. The fertile land nurtured the grapes. New varieties of grapes were developed and new ideas and technology changed the simple beginnings into a vast industry. The ability to transport incredibly large quantities of food across the country has resulted in a unique degree of uniformity in many American foods. Fruit and vegetables are harvested before the sun has brought them to the peak of perfection and they continue to ripen on the way to market. Bold flavors tend to be muted for the mass market. Yet, though the national yellow waxy cheeses of America are consumed by the ton, cheeses of incomparable quality are also made in America. And though convenience foods are bought in ever greater quantities, the interest and enthusiasm for homemade foods is also increasing.

As food has become more expensive, there has been a return to the pleasure of cooking, and recipes once prepared by mothers and grandmothers are being rediscovered and prepared with joy and satisfaction.

Soups

Cioppino

6 servings

- 2 *dozen clams*
- $^1/_2$ *cup dried Italian mushrooms*
- $^1/_3$ *cup olive oil*
- 2 *medium sized onions, finely chopped*
- 2 *cloves garlic, crushed*
- 1 *large green pepper, seeded and chopped*
- 4 *medium sized tomatoes, peeled, seeded and chopped*
- 2 *cups red wine*
- $1^1/_2$ *teaspoons salt Freshly ground black pepper*
- 1 *teaspoon oregano*
- 2 *tablespoons tomato paste*
- 1 *($1^1/_2$ pound) lobster or crab, cut into pieces*
- 1 *pound shrimp, shelled and deveined*
- 1 *(2 to $2^1/_2$ pound) striped bass, filleted and sliced crosswise.*

Scrub the clams thoroughly. In a large pot, bring about 1 inch of water to a boil. Add the clams, cover and cook over medium heat 5 to 7 minutes until the shells open. Discard any shells that do not open. Strain the clam broth through several layers of cheesecloth and reserve 2 cups. Set the clams aside in their shells. Soak the dried mushrooms in warm water 30 minutes. Heat the olive oil in a large casserole. Add the onions, garlic, green pepper and mushrooms and sauté 5 minutes over medium heat. Add the tomatoes, red wine, reserved clam broth, salt, pepper, oregano and tomato paste. Cover and simmer 30 minutes. Add the lobster pieces and cook 5 minutes. Add the shrimp and striped bass and cook 5 minutes more. Add the clams and cook about 3 minutes until heated through. Serve the Cioppino from the casserole with a green salad and plenty of warm sourdough bread.

Oyster stew

6 servings

- 1 *quart shucked oysters with their liquor*
- 2 *tablespoons butter*
- 2 *cups hot milk*
- 2 *cups hot light cream*
- $^1/_2$ *teaspoon salt Freshly ground black pepper Paprika*

Put the oysters with their liquor and butter in a saucepan. Heat gently for about 5 minutes until the oysters grow round and plump and the edges begin to curl. Remove from the heat and add the hot milk and cream. Season with salt, pepper and paprika.
Serve immediately with oyster crackers.
In Roman times the senators were elected by counting the names scratched into the inner surface of oyster shells. Oysters have always been secretive.

Pumpkin soup

8 servings

- 1 *pound pumpkin or 1 (1 pound) can pumpkin purée*
- 2 *medium sized potatoes, peeled*
- 3 *cups milk*
- 3 *cups chicken broth*
- $^3/_4$ *teaspoon salt Freshly ground black pepper*
- 1 *teaspoon sugar*
- 1 *teaspoon nutmeg*
- $^1/_2$ *teaspoon ground ginger*
- $^1/_2$ *cup sour cream*

Cook the pumpkin and potatoes in plenty of boiling salted water 30 minutes or until tender. Drain, cut into pieces and place in the jar of an electric blender. Add 2 cups milk and blend until smooth. Place the pumpkin purée in a large saucepan and add the remaining milk, chicken broth, salt, pepper, sugar, nutmeg and ginger. Bring to a boil, stirring constantly. Lower the heat and simmer the soup 5 minutes. Ladle into individual soup bowls and garnish each serving with 1 tablespoon sour cream.

Cream of asparagus soup

6 servings

> 1 *pound fresh asparagus*
> 1 *small yellow onion,*
> *finely chopped*
> 2 *tablespoons butter*
> 2 *tablespoons flour*
> 5 *cups chicken broth*
> $^1/_2$ *teaspoon salt*
> *Freshly ground black*
> *pepper*
> $^1/_2$ *cup heavy cream*
> *Grated rind of 2 lemons*

Discard the bottom inch of each asparagus spear. Wash the spears carefully in plenty of cold water to remove any sand. Cut into 2 inch lengths.

Fry the onion in hot butter for 3 minutes until softened. Stir in the flour and add the chicken broth gradually. Add the asparagus. Cover the saucepan and simmer over low heat for 20 minutes until the asparagus is tender. Purée the soup in blender and then force it through a strainer to remove any 'strings'.

Return the soup to a clean saucepan. Taste it and add salt and pepper if necessary. Add the cream and bring to boiling point. Garnish the soup with freshly grated lemon rind.

Asparagus soup heralds the spring and is at its best at the height of the asparagus season. It can be served either hot or cold and also garnished with either croutons or cooked asparagus tips.

Beef and barley soup

6 servings

> 3 *pounds marrow soup bones*
> *with meat clinging to*
> *the bones*
> 2 *onions, peeled and roughly*
> *chopped*
> 2 *carrots, washed and*
> *chopped*
> 2 *stalks celery, chopped*
> 2 *bay leaves*
> 1 *teaspoon thyme*
> 1 *teaspoon peppercorns*
> 4 *sprigs parsley*
> 3 *quarts water*
> 2 *pounds boneless chuck*
> *steak or beef brisket*
> 1 *teaspoon salt*
> *Freshly ground black*
> *pepper*
> $^1/_2$ *cup pearl barley*

Place the bones in a heavy roasting pan and roast uncovered in their own fat in a preheated 350° oven for 15 minutes. Add the onions, carrots and celery and allow them to brown for an additional 10 minutes. Transfer the bones and vegetables into a large soup pot. Add 1 cup water to the roasting pan and scrape up the brown pieces clinging to the bottom of the pan. Add this flavored liquid to the soup pot. Add the bay leaves, thyme, peppercorns, parsley and water. Simmer over gentle heat for 2 hours, skimming the surface of the broth occasionally. Adjust the lid so the pan is almost covered. Add the beef and continue simmering for 2 hours. Remove the beef and cut into small pieces. Strain the broth. Discard the bones and vegetables. Chill the broth overnight to allow the fat to rise to the surface. Skim off the fat. Pour the broth into a clean saucepan. Bring to simmering point and add the salt, pepper and barley. Cover and simmer for 20 minutes. Add the beef and continue cooking for 10 minutes.

Chicken soup

6 servings

> 1 *(2 to 2$^1/_2$ pound)*
> *chicken, quartered*
> 1 *onion, cut into wedges*
> 1 *carrot, peeled and sliced*
> 1 *stalk celery, sliced*
> 1 *bay leaf*
> $^1/_2$ *teaspoon thyme*
> 8 *peppercorns*
> 8 *cups water*
> $^1/_2$ *cup rice*
> 2 *carrots, peeled and cut into*
> *2 inch long strips*
> $^1/_2$ *teaspoon sage*
> 1 *teaspoon salt*
> *Freshly ground black pepper*
> $^1/_2$ *cup heavy cream*

Place the chicken, onion, sliced carrot, celery, bay leaf, thyme, peppercorns and water in a large saucepan. Bring to a boil, lower the heat and simmer, covered, 45 minutes. Remove the 4 pieces of chicken from the broth and set aside until cool enough to handle. Separate the meat from the skin and bones and reserve. Return the skin and bones to the broth. Cover and simmer 1$^1/_2$ hours more. Strain the broth and refrigerate several hours or overnight. Discard the fat on the surface of the broth. Place the broth in a saucepan and bring to a boil. Stir in the rice, carrots, sage, salt and pepper. Lower the heat, cover and simmer 20 minutes. Dice the reserved chicken meat. Add the meat and cream to the soup and simmer 10 minutes more.
Serve immediately.

New Englanders make clam chowder with milk. In Manhattan, they add tomatoes. Either way, the clams are barely cooked through, so that they will stay sweet and tender.

New England clam chowder

6 servings

1 quart soft shell
  steamer clams or
  2 (8 ounce) cans minced
  clams
3 small potatoes, peeled and
  diced
3 slices bacon, cut
  into small pieces
1 medium sized yellow
  onion, finely chopped
3 cups milk
1 cup heavy cream
1 tablespoon butter
  Salt if necessary
  Freshly ground black
  pepper

Scrub clams and soak them in three changes of cold water to remove the sand. Steam the clams over 1 cup water for 8 minutes until the shells open. Discard the shells and chop clams into small pieces. Strain the broth through cheesecloth to remove any sand.
Boil the potatoes in salted water for 15 minutes.
Fry the bacon in a saucepan until 1 tablespoon of fat has rendered. Remove the bacon. Fry the onion for 3 minutes in bacon fat. Add the strained clam broth or broth from canned clams. Simmer for 5 minutes. Add chopped clams, milk, cream, butter and potatoes. Season with salt. Simmer for 5 minutes until potatoes are just tender. Garnish bowls with a sprinkling of freshly ground black pepper and reserved bacon.

There are no rules to making vegetable soup. Almost any vegetable in season can be simmered in a hearty beef broth to make a beautiful soup for the evening.

Vegetable soup

8 servings

2 tablespoons butter
1 medium sized yellow onion, finely chopped
2 carrots, peeled and diced
2 stalks celery, diced
8 cups beef broth
2 medium sized potatoes, diced
1 cup string beans, cut into small pieces
$^1/_2$ cup peas
3 medium sized tomatoes, chopped
$^1/_2$ teaspoon salt
Freshly ground black pepper
2 tablespoons finely chopped parsley

Heat the butter in a saucepan. Add the onion, carrots and celery. Fry over low heat for 10 minutes. Add the beef broth and potatoes. Simmer for 10 minutes and add the beans. Simmer 5 minutes and add the peas, tomatoes, salt and pepper. Cook over low heat for another 5 minutes. Garnish with parsley just before serving.
This winter family soup is bursting with flavors. Add as many other fresh vegetables as your pot will hold and serve with crusty bread.

Sauces

Mayonnaise

Makes 1 pint

  4 *egg yolks*
$^1/_2$ *teaspoon salt*
  1 *teaspoon mild mustard*
     Juice of 1 lemon
  2 *cups salad oil*

Place the egg yolks, salt and
mustard in the bowl of an electric
mixer. Beat until the yolks are
very thick. Add the strained juice
of $^1/_2$ lemon. Beat at top speed
until very thick. Add $^1/_4$ cup of
oil literally a drop at a time.
Continue adding the oil very
slowly until 1 cup of oil has been
used. Add remaining lemon juice
and 1 tablespoon of hot water if
the mayonnaise is too thick to
beat. Add the remaining oil
gradually. Taste the mayonnaise
and add more salt or lemon juice
if necessary. Fill a glass jar and
store, covered, in the refrigerator.

Spaghetti sauce

6 servings

  2 *tablespoons oil*
  1 *onion, finely chopped*
  1 *clove garlic, crushed*
  1 *green pepper, finely*
     chopped
  4 *medium sized mushrooms,*
     sliced
$^3/_4$ *pound ground beef*
  2 *ripe tomatoes, finely*
     chopped
  2 *teaspoons tomato paste*
  1 *bay leaf*
  1 *teaspoon oregano*
  1 *teaspoon salt*
     Freshly ground black
     pepper
  1 *cup beef broth*

Heat the oil in a large skillet. Add
the onion, garlic and green
pepper and fry for 3 minutes.
Add the mushrooms and fry for 2
minutes. Stir in the beef and cook
over moderate heat until
browned. Add all the remaining
ingredients and simmer,
uncovered over moderately low
heat for 45 minutes until almost
all of the liquid has evaporated.
Serve with spaghetti.

Tomato sauce

$1^1/_2$ *pounds red summer ripe*
     tomatoes
  2 *tablespoons olive oil*
  1 *onion, chopped*
  2 *cloves garlic, crushed*
  1 *small carrot, finely chopped*
  4 *sprigs parsley*
  1 *bay leaf*
$^1/_2$ *teaspoon marjoram,*
     basil or oregano
$^1/_2$ *teaspoon salt*
     Freshly ground black
     pepper
$^1/_2$ *cup chicken broth*

Cut the tomatoes into small
pieces. Heat the oil in a saucepan
and fry the onion, garlic and
carrot for 5 minutes. Add the
tomatoes and all the remaining
ingredients. Cover and simmer
over low heat for 20 minutes.
Force the sauce through a
strainer. Serve with fish, chicken
or meat loaf.
Note: In the winter the tomatoes
will not have enough flavor, so
use canned tomatoes and add 1
teaspoon tomato paste.

Hollandaise sauce

6 servings

 12 *tablespoons butter*
  3 *egg yolks*
$^1/_2$ *teaspoon salt*
     Dash of cayenne pepper
     Juice of 1 lemon

Reserve 2 tablespoons cold
butter and heat remaining butter
in a small saucepan until hot, but
not boiling.
Combine in a small saucepan,
the egg yolks, salt, pepper and
the juice of half a lemon. Place
pan over gentle heat. Add 1
tablespoon cold reserved butter
and stir constantly until the
butter has melted. Add
remaining tablespoon of cold
butter and continue stirring until
melted.
Remove the pan from the heat
and stir in hot butter gradually.
Continue stirring until a thick
sauce has formed. Add
remaining lemon juice to taste
and more salt and pepper if
necessary.

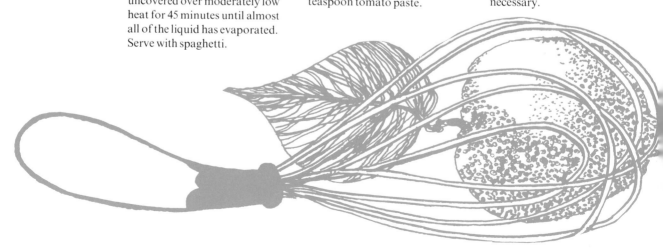

Meat dishes

Steak

Columbus brought the first cattle to the New World but the meat was so tough that most people preferred to eat wild buffalo. It was not until the colonists brought their own livestock from England and Scotland that Americans began their continuing love affair with beef. More cattle were subsequently brought from other countries, and the Texas Longhorns, English Herefords, Aberdeen Angus and French Charolais have been bred and cross-bred until now America can rightfully boast of having the largest supply of good quality beef of any country in the world. Vast cattle ranches in the southwest provide almost unlimited grazing ground until the animals are ready to be fattened on grain and corn from the midwest.
Beef is by far the most popular meat in America and, in spite of rising prices, rare is the family that does not eat beef at least once a week. The choice of cuts of beef is vast, ranging from a proud roast or tender juicy steak to a flavorful stew, a hamburger or simply a corned beef sandwich on rye bread.
Unlike most European countries, veal is in much less demand than beef. It is more economical for the farmer to fatten the calves until they are sold as baby beef than to offer milk fed veal. Consequently veal is not always readily available in small towns and the price everywhere is very high.
Pork is the second choice after beef. Spareribs and roast pork are always welcome treats for dinner. When all the pork has been eaten, there is ham and bacon and two hundred varieties of sausage. Virginia claims to produce the best of all hams. To be a Virginia ham, the pampered pigs are fed first on peanuts and then on corn. They are then smoked tenderly over oak and hickory chips.
Lamb has never achieved great popularity in America and most of it is sold to its loyal devotees on the east coast.

6 servings

6 individual steaks, 1 inch thick
1 teaspoon salt
Freshly ground black pepper
Mushroom sauce

Select steaks of uniform thickness. The meat should be well marbled and should be dark red to insure tenderness. A piece of bright red meat with no streaks of fat is almost guaranteed to be tough. Shell or rib eye steaks are good choices for broiling or grilling. Brush your broiler pan or grill rack with oil. Preheat the broiler or prepare a hot charcoal fire. Broil or grill the steaks 3 to 4 minutes on each side about 3 inches from the flame. For a medium or well done steak, increase the total cooking time 3 to 5 minutes. Sprinkle the steaks on both sides with salt and pepper and serve with mushroom sauce.

Mushroom sauce for steak:
$^1/_2$ pound mushrooms
2 tablespoons butter
2 scallions, finely chopped
3 tablespoons flour
1 teaspoon paprika
$1^1/_2$ cups beef broth
$^1/_4$ teaspoon salt
Freshly ground black pepper
Juice of 1 lemon

Separate the mushroom caps and stems. Slice the caps thinly and chop the stems finely. Melt the butter and sauté the scallions over high heat until softened. Add the mushrooms and sauté about 2 minutes, stirring gently with a wooden spoon. Sprinkle in the flour and paprika and cook, stirring, 1 to 2 minutes. Add the broth, stirring constantly until the sauce thickens. Season with salt, pepper and lemon juice.

Sea captain's wives in Salem, Massachussetts prepared a New England boiled dinner to welcome their husbands home, in the early days of our country – much as modern wives and mothers celebrate their returning men with steaks and ice cream.

New England boiled dinner

6 servings

2¹/₂ pounds corned beef or beef
    brisket
  4 cups water
  1 bay leaf
  1 teaspoon thyme
  3 sprigs parsley
  1 teaspoon peppercorns
  2 onions, sliced
  2 carrots, sliced
  2 stalks celery, sliced

Accompaniments:

  1 small cabbage, cut into
    wedges
  5 carrots, sliced
  6 potatoes, halved wedges
  3 parsnips, cut into cubes
  1 small turnip, cut into cubes

Dressing.

  1 cup heavy cream
  3 tablespoons prepared
    horseradish
    Juice of ¹/₂ lemon

Place the beef in a casserole. Add enough water to just cover the beef. Add herbs and the first group of vegetables. Cover and simmer over low heat for 2¹/₂ hours until the beef is tender. Tie each cabbage wedge with a piece of string so it will retain its shape. Cook the vegetables in separate saucepans in salted simmering water for 15 to 20 minutes until each is cooked. Drain the vegetables and remove the string from the cabbage wedges. Whip the cream and combine with horseradish and lemon juice. Serve the horseradish dressing separately.

Hamburgers – it is not whether you serve them, it is how to vary them. Try tomato and green pepper, sharp cheddar cheese, sour cream with dill or mix in chili powder or mustard. These and other ideas on page 22.

Hamburgers

Beef stew with beer

6 servings

- 2 *pounds lean ground chuck*
- 1 *teaspoon Worcestershire sauce*
- 2 *tablespoons bottled steak sauce*
- $^1/_2$ *teaspoon salt*
- $^1/_2$ *teaspoon cracked pepper*
- 2 *tablespoons red wine or beef broth or water*
- 1 *tablespoon oil*

Combine all the ingredients in a bowl except the oil, and form into 6 patties. Try not to be motherly with the hamburger, neither patting it approvingly nor absentmindedly. In fact, handle it as little as possible as the meat will become compact and the outside will look like a burnt offering, while the inside will quiver with raw coldness. Broil or pan fry the hamburgers in the oil for 4 minutes on each side.

Variations: A sophisticated hamburger can be made by adding 2 tablespoons gin, 2 tablespoons of sesame seeds, 1 chopped tomato and $^1/_2$ teaspoon basil to 2 pounds ground chuck. Barbecued hamburgers are made by adding $^1/_3$ cup barbecue sauce, see recipe on page 25, to 2 pounds ground beef. Cheeseburgers are made using the basic hamburger recipe on this page. A slice of cheddar cheese is placed on top of the patty after it has been turned. Chinese hamburgers are made by adding 1 tablespoon soy sauce, 1 teaspoon chinese mustard, 2 tablespoons tomato catsup and 1 tablespoon sherry to the ground beef.

To make hamburgers with dill and sour cream add a garnish of 1 teaspoon dill weed and sour cream to the basic recipe. Lemon juice can replace Worcestershire sauce.

Finally, hamburger meat, unlike certain wines, does not improve with age and so it should be cooked as soon as possible.

6 servings

- $2^1/_2$ *pounds boneless chuck, cut into cubes*
- 3 *tablespoons oil*
- 4 *yellow onions, sliced*
- 2 *cloves garlic, crushed*
- 3 *tablespoons flour*
- 1 *(12 ounce) can beer*
- $^1/_2$ *cup beef broth*
- 1 *teaspoon sugar*
- 1 *teaspoon salt*
  Freshly ground black pepper
- $^1/_4$ *teaspoon nutmeg*

Bouquet Garni:

- 3 *sprigs parsley*
- 1 *bay leaf*
- 1 *teaspoon peppercorns*
- $^1/_2$ *teaspoon thyme*

- 6 *slices French bread or 6 rounds firm bread*
- 2 *tablespoons mild mustard*

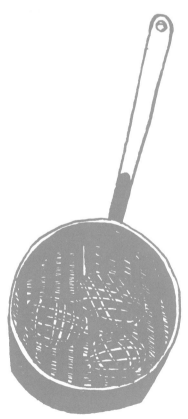

Brown the beef on all sides in a skillet in hot oil. Transfer the beef to a casserole and fry the onions and garlic in the same oil for 3 minutes until softened. Stir in the flour and add the beer and beef broth gradually. Season with sugar, salt, pepper and nutmeg and transfer to the casserole. Tie the bouquet garni ingredients into a piece of cheesecloth and bury the bag among the beef cubes. Cover the casserole and place in a preheated 350° oven for $1\frac{1}{2}$ hours. Discard the bouquet garni and chill the casserole overnight in the refrigerator.

When ready to serve, reheat the covered casserole in a 350° oven for 20 minutes. Coat the bread with mustard and push it, mustard side down, into the sauce until the bread is half covered. Return the casserole to the oven and continue cooking, uncovered, for 15 minutes until the surface of the bread is crisp and lightly browned.

This is an excellent party dish and always a success.

Broiled flank steak

4 servings

2 *pounds flank steak*

Marinade:
1 *onion, finely chopped*
1 *clove garlic, crushed*
2 *tablespoons soy sauce*
$^1/_2$ *cup red wine*
1 *tablespoon vegetable oil*
Freshly ground black pepper

Draw criss cross lines in the steak with a sharp knife to cut the surface fibers. Combine the marinade ingredients. Place the steak flat in a shallow enamel or glass baking dish. Add the combined marinade ingredients. Cover the dish and marinate the beef for 12 hours in the refrigerator. Turn the beef once. Remove the beef from the marinade. Broil 4 minutes on each side, as close to the broiler as possible. To carve, hold the knife almost flat and parallel to the beef. Cut long thin slices of beef across the grain. Serve with broiled tomatoes, a green vegetable and French fried potatoes.
Note: If you do not have time to marinate the beef for 12 hours, even 1 hour will tenderize and improve the flavor of the steak.

Meat loaf

6 servings

2 *tablespoons butter*
2 *onions, finely chopped*
1 *clove garlic, crushed*
3 *stalks celery, chopped*
2 *pounds ground beef or*
  2 pounds of assorted
  ground meats, i.e.
  pork, lamb and beef
1 *cup freshly made*
  breadcrumbs
1 *teaspoon marjoram*
$^1/_2$ *teaspoon cinnamon*
2 *tablespoons finely*
  chopped parsley
1 *tablespoon tomato paste*
1 *egg, lightly beaten*
$^1/_4$ *cup beef broth or red wine*
6 *slices uncooked bacon*

Heat the butter and fry the onions, garlic and celery for 3 minutes until softened. Add the ground beef and cook for 10 minutes until lightly browned. Pour off all the accumulated fat. Remove from heat and combine with all the remaining ingredients except the bacon. Place in a buttered loaf pan. Cover with the strips of bacon. Bake uncovered in the center of a preheated 350° oven for 1 hour. Serve with tomato sauce, recipe on page 18 or mushroom sauce, recipe on page 19.

Pepper steak

4 servings

4 *(1 inch thick) fillet steaks*
1 *tablespoon oil*
$1^1/_2$ *tablespoons cracked pepper*
2 *tablespoons butter*
1 *teaspoon salt*
$^1/_4$ *cup brandy*
$^1/_4$ *cup heavy cream*

Brush each steak with oil. Press cracked pepper onto the surface of both sides of the steak, using the heel of your hand.
Heat the butter in a skillet. Sauté the steaks over high heat 4 minutes on each side. Take care not to let the butter burn. The surface of the steaks should be brown and crusty while the center remains rare. Season the steaks with salt.
Add the brandy and touch it with a lighted match. When the flames die down, transfer the steaks to a hot serving plate. Add the cream to the skillet and boil over high heat for 2 minutes. Pour over the steaks and serve immediately.
The addition of cream to many recipes acts like a soft pedal on the piano. It mutes the flavor and gently unifies the dish.

Chili

4 servings

2 *tablespoons butter*
1 *onion, finely chopped*
2 *cloves garlic, crushed*
1 *green pepper, chopped*
$1^1/_2$ *pounds ground beef*
2 *to 3 tablespoons chili powder*
  Dash of cayenne pepper
  Dash of tabasco sauce
1 *(8 ounce) can Italian plum tomatoes*
2 *(8 ounce) cans tomato sauce*
1 *teaspoon salt*
1 *teaspoon sugar*
2 *bay leaves*
1 *(8 ounce) can red kidney beans, rinsed under cold water*

Heat the butter in a large skillet. Add the onion, garlic and green pepper and cook over moderate heat for 3 minutes. Add the ground beef and continue cooking until lightly browned. Stir in all the remaining ingredients except the kidney beans. Simmer, uncovered, for 40 minutes. Add the kidney beans and continue cooking for 10 minutes. Discard the bay leaves and serve with crusty bread, a tossed salad and a large mug of foaming beer.

The tantalizing fragrance of barbecued spareribs cooked on an outdoor grill is an invitation for all the neighbors to come over with plenty of cold beer, and praise the host's special barbeque sauce.

Crown roast of pork

8 servings

    8 pounds loin of pork
       (16 pork chops) in 1 piece
    4 tablespoons butter
    1 onion, finely chopped
    2 stalks celery, finely chopped
  1/2 pound mild pork sausage
       meat
    2 cups freshly made
       breadcrumbs
    1 teaspoon rosemary
    2 tablespoons finely
       chopped parsley
  1/2 teaspoon thyme
    1 teaspoon salt
       Freshly ground black
       pepper
  1/4 cup chicken broth

Ask the butcher to scrape the fat from the top part of the ribs, crack the bones to facilitate carving and tie the loin into a crown. Brush the pork with melted butter and place in a roasting pan. Wrap pieces of foil around each bone end to prevent burning.

To prepare the stuffing, heat the remaining butter in a skillet. Add the onion and celery. Fry for 3 minutes until softened. Stir in the sausage meat and continue cooking over low heat until all the fat has rendered. Remove from the heat and drain off the fat. Stir in the remaining ingredients and fill into the center of the pork circle. Cover with a piece of foil. Roast uncovered in a preheated 350° oven allowing 30 minutes to each pound.

Fill the crown with freshly cooked green peas. Garnish with spiced apples and serve with roast potatoes.

Barbecued spareribs

8 servings

    1 cup cider vinegar
  1/2 cup water or pineapple juice
    1 cup sugar
    2 cloves garlic, crushed
  1/4 cup sherry
  1/4 cup soy sauce
    1 tablespoon cornstarch
       dissolved in
    2 tablespoons water
    6 pounds spareribs

Place the vinegar, water and sugar in a saucepan. Boil for 2 minutes until syrupy. Add garlic, sherry and soy sauce and simmer for 3 minutes. Stir in cornstarch paste and continue cooking for 2 minutes until the sauce has thickened. Cool the sauce.

Cut the spareribs between each rib, cutting almost through the length but keep the pieces attached so that they can be turned easily. Marinate the ribs in the sauce for 2 hours. Roast, uncovered, for 1 hour in a preheated 350° oven. Turn the ribs every 20 minutes. Baste the ribs with the barbecue sauce every 10 minutes.

The barbecue sauce can also be used for chicken. The spareribs can be cooked over charcoal on an outdoor grill.

Crisp pork chops with peaches

4 servings

8 *center cut pork chops*
¹/₂ *cup flour seasoned with*
   1 teaspoon salt
   Freshly ground black
   pepper
   1 teaspoon dry mustard
   powder
2 *eggs, lightly beaten*
³/₄ *cup freshly made*
   breadcrumbs
1 *tablespoon oil*
2 *tablespoons butter*
1 *(1 pound) can peaches*
1 *teaspoon mild mustard*
1 *teaspoon lemon juice*
4 *sprigs parsley*

Dredge the pork chops with seasoned flour. Dip in beaten egg and finally press into the breadcrumbs. Heat the oil and butter in a large skillet and fry the pork chops 10 minutes on each side. In the meantime, drain the peaches and reserve the juice. Place ¹/₂ cup peach juice in a saucepan. Stir in the mustard and lemon juice. Add the peaches and simmer over low heat for 5 minutes. Serve the pork chops with a garnish of peaches and parsley sprigs. Pour the peach sauce over the peaches.

Pork loin with apples

6 servings

3 *pounds boneless pork loin*
2 *tablespoons butter*
1 *onion, finely chopped*
1 *clove garlic, crushed*
1 *green pepper, chopped*
2 *apples, peeled, cored and*
   sliced
1 *teaspoon cumin powder*
2 *tablespoons flour*
1¹/₂ *cups chicken broth*
¹/₂ *teaspoon salt*
   Freshly ground black
   pepper
1 *tablespoon mild mustard*
2 *tablespoons finely chopped*
   parsley

Cut the pork into 1¹/₂ inch cubes. Brown the pork in hot butter and add the onion, garlic, green pepper and apples. Continue cooking for 3 minutes. Stir in the cumin powder and cook for 1 minute. Stir in the flour. Add the broth, salt, pepper and mustard. Cover and simmer for 30 minutes until the pork is tender. Garnish with parsley and serve on a bed of rice.

Veal cutlets

6 servings

2¹/₂ *pounds veal cut from the leg*
   into 2 thick steaks
2 *to 3 cloves garlic*
3 *tablespoons butter*
6 *mushrooms, quartered*
3 *tablespoons flour*
1¹/₂ *cups chicken broth*
2 *oranges*
¹/₂ *teaspoon salt*
   Freshly ground black
   pepper
2 *tablespoons sherry*
2 *tablespoons finely chopped*
   parsley

Cut each veal steak into 3 equal sized pieces. Cut the garlic into thin slivers. Make several small cuts in the veal with the point of a sharp knife. Insert the garlic slivers into the cuts. Heat the butter in a large skillet and sauté the veal, 2 pieces at a time, until lightly browned. Arrange the veal in a baking dish. Sauté the mushrooms in the same butter for 3 minutes. Stir in the flour and add the chicken broth gradually to form a smooth mushroom sauce. Grate the orange rind and add to the sauce. Add the salt, pepper and sherry. Pour half of the sauce over the veal. Cover the dish with aluminium foil and bake in a preheated 375° oven for 30 minutes. Keep the remaining sauce warm. In the meantime remove the remaining white pith from the oranges and slice them thinly. Place the oranges in a bowl. Cover the bowl with a plate and place over simmering water for 10 minutes. Spoon the remaining sauce over the veal. Garnish with hot orange slices and chopped parsley. Serve on a bed of spinach or egg noodles.

Veal scallopini

6 servings

- 4 tablespoons butter
- 1 1/2 pounds veal scallopini
- 1 teaspoon salt
  Freshly ground black pepper
- 2 scallions, thinly sliced
- 3 tomatoes, peeled, seeded and cut into strips
- 1 1/2 cups thinly sliced mushrooms
- 1 1/2 cups chicken broth
- 1/2 teaspoon oregano

Heat the butter in a large skillet and sauté the veal quickly on both sides over high heat. Remove from the pan, sprinkle with 1/2 teaspoon salt and pepper and keep warm while preparing the sauce. Add the scallions to the skillet and sauté 2 minutes. Add the tomatoes and mushrooms and cook, stirring, 4 to 5 minutes. Add the broth, oregano and remaining salt and pepper and bring to a boil. Simmer 4 to 5 minutes. Return the veal to the pan and baste with the sauce. Serve with rice and a crisp green salad.

Ham with sherry

6 servings

- 4 cups ground ham
- 2 cups cooked rice
- 2 tomatoes, peeled, seeded and chopped
- 1/4 cup finely chopped green pepper
- 1 small onion, finely chopped
- 2 eggs
- 1 teaspoon prepared (Dijon type) mustard
- 1 teaspoon Worcestershire sauce
- 1/2 cup dry sherry
- 1/2 cup heavy cream
- 1 cup freshly made breadcrumbs
- 1/4 cup melted butter
- 1/2 teaspoon paprika

Combine the ham, rice, tomatoes, green pepper and onion in a mixing bowl. In a separate bowl, beat the eggs with the mustard and Worcestershire sauce. Add the sherry and cream and combine thoroughly. Add the liquid ingredients to the ham mixture and place in a buttered casserole. Toss the breadcrumbs with the butter and sprinkle over the ham mixture. Dust the breadcrumbs with paprika. Bake, uncovered, in a preheated 350° oven 45 minutes. Serve from the casserole.

Ham steak with cranberries

4 servings

- 4 ham steaks
- 2 tablespoons butter
- 2 teaspoons mild mustard
  Freshly ground black pepper
- 1 cup cranberries
- 1 cup sugar
  Grated rind and juice of 1 orange

Place the ham steaks on a broiler rack. Melt the butter and stir in the mustard and pepper. Brush the ham with flavored butter. Broil the ham 5 minutes on each side until tender. In the meantime, wash the cranberries and place in a skillet. Add the sugar, grated orange rind and juice. Toss the ingredients together gently. Allow the cranberries to stand undisturbed for 5 minutes. Place over low heat and simmer for 5 minutes until the cranberries are hot and shiny. There is only a small amount of liquid with the cranberries, so take care not to let them burn.
Serve the ham with noodles and garnish with glazed cranberries.

If any glazed ham is left over from dinner, it will certainly disappear in sandwiches the next day.

Glazed ham

8 servings

> 6 *pounds oven ready fully cooked ham*
> 2 *cups orange juice or cider*
> 1 *cup apricot preserves*
> 2 *tablespoons sherry*
> 2 *tablespoons mild mustard*

Ask the butcher to remove the skin from the ham and score the fat in a diamond pattern. Place the ham on a roasting rack, fat side up, and pour the orange juice or cider into the roasting pan. Place in the center of a preheated 350° oven and bake, uncovered, for 3 hours. Allow 30 minutes cooking time to the pound. One hour before the total cooking time has elapsed, prepare the glaze. Heat the apricot preserves in a small saucepan and force them through a strainer to remove the skins. Stir in the sherry and mustard. Brush the ham with the glaze every fifteen minutes for the last hour.

The bone is removed from the leg of lamb so it is easy to serve. The slices arrive hot, juicy and fragrant with herbs.

Roast leg of lamb

6 servings

- 6 *slices bread with crusts removed*
- 3 *tablespoons finely chopped parsley*
- 3 *tablespoons chopped chives*
- 2 *teaspoons thyme*
- 1 *teaspoon rosemary*
- 2 *cloves garlic, crushed*
- 1 *teaspoon salt*
  Freshly ground black pepper
- ³/₄ *cup whole shelled pistachio nuts*
- 4 *pound leg of lamb with the bone removed*
- 2 *tablespoons butter, melted*

Put 2 slices of bread, the herbs, the garlic, salt and pepper into a blender. Blend until breadcrumbs are formed and the herbs are finely chopped. Add the pistachio nuts and spread the mixture onto the inner surface of the lamb. Roll the lamb and tie with string at 2 inch intervals. Make breadcrumbs from the remaining bread. Roll the lamb firmly in the crumbs, covering the surface evenly. Place the lamb on a roasting rack and drizzle the melted butter over the lamb. Roast, uncovered, in a preheated 350° oven for 2 hours, allowing 30 minutes to the pound. Wrap the lamb in aluminum foil and allow it to rest for 20 minutes before slicing.

Lamb stew

6 servings

- 6 *pounds lamb shanks*
- 3 *tablespoons oil*
- 1 *onion, finely chopped*
- 2 *cloves garlic, crushed*
- 2 *carrots, finely chopped*
- 2 *stalks celery, sliced*
- 1¹/₂ *cups dried split peas*
- 3¹/₂ *cups beef broth*
- 1 *teaspoon salt*
  Freshly ground black pepper

Brown the lamb shanks on all sides in hot oil. Transfer to a large casserole. Fry the onion, garlic, carrots and celery in the same oil for 3 minutes and add to casserole. Add the split peas, beef broth, salt and pepper. Cover and cook in a preheated 350° oven for 2 hours. The peas will absorb almost all the liquid. This simply prepared stew makes an excellent, hearty dinner for a cold winter night. **Note:** Much of the weight of the lamb shanks is in the bones. If there are any leftovers, remove the lamb from the bones, add another cup or two of beef broth and serve as a soup.

Poultry dishes

Chicken is a favorite food all over America as well as the rest of the world. It is roasted and fried, stewed, poached, braised, barbecued and boiled in a thousand different ways. It combines so well with such a variety of other foods that its versatility is seemingly limitless. In America, as in many other countries, it has long been a symbol of prosperity. Henry IV of France began the idea of a chicken for very pot, and the nobility of the notion enabled this hope to last until Franklin Roosevelt's time. Now, thanks to mass production, chicken is less of a luxury and more of an everyday food.
Part of the virtue of chicken is its economy. The legs can appear one day as southern fried chicken and the next day the breasts are poached and served with a cream sauce. The bones are made into the soup and the giblets become a gravy. Chicken livers can be stored in the freezer until there are enough to make a pâté.
It is fairly easy to tell the age and quality of the chicken by simply looking at the way it is sitting. If it is plump and white, with its skin fitting its body, then tuck it under your arm and take it home. The breast bone will be flexible and the joints, when cut, will be bright red. Chickens are best cooked as soon as possible. If there is no time to cook a chicken, America is dotted across its length and breadth with roadside franchised stands that will obligingly cook it at the drop of a deep fryer.

Creamed turkey

6 servings

- 3 tablespoons butter
- 1 small onion, finely chopped
- 1 1/2 cups sliced mushrooms
- 4 tablespoons flour
- 1 1/2 cups turkey or chicken broth
- 1 1/2 cups heavy cream
- 1/2 teaspoon salt
  Freshly ground black pepper
- 3/4 teaspoon rosemary
  Juice of 1 lemon
- 3 to 4 cups leftover turkey, cut into strips

Heat the butter in a large saucepan and sauté the onion until softened. Add the mushrooms and sauté 2 minutes. Add the flour and cook, stirring, 1 minute. Add the broth and cream gradually, stirring constantly until the sauce thickens. Stir in the salt, pepper, rosemary, lemon juice and turkey and simmer 5 minutes. Serve over rice or on triangles of toasted bread.

Crisp cornish hens

4 servings

- 4 Cornish hens
- 1 cup flour seasoned with 1 teaspoon salt
  Freshly ground black pepper
- 2 eggs, lightly beaten
- 1 1/2 cups freshly made breadcrumbs
  Oil or shortening for deep frying

Truss the Cornish hens. Roll each hen first in seasoned flour, then in beaten egg and finally in breadcrumbs. Heat the oil and fry each hen for about 8 minutes until crisp and browned on all sides. Drain on paper towels. Place the hens in 2 baking dishes and roast, uncovered, in a preheated 350° oven for 30 minutes until tender. Serve with Hollandaise sauce (on page 18), combined with 1 tablespoon tomato paste.

Dove in red wine

4 servings

- 8 doves
- 2 tablespoons butter
- 1 tablespoon oil
- 1 small onion, finely chopped
- 2 carrots, finely chopped
- 1 stalk celery, finely chopped
- 2 tablespoons flour
- 1 cup red wine
- 1/2 cup chicken broth
- 1 teaspoon prepared mild mustard
- 1 teaspoon tomato paste
- 2 tomatoes, peeled, seeded and chopped
- 1 teaspoon oregano
- 1/2 teaspoon salt
  Freshly ground black pepper
- 2 tablespoons finely chopped parsley

Brown the doves in hot combined butter and oil and transfer to a large casserole. Fry the onion, carrots and celery in the same butter. Stir in the flour and add the wine gradually. Add the chicken broth and all the remaining ingredients except the parsley. Cover and cook in a preheated 425° oven for 35 minutes until the doves are tender. Garnish with parsley and serve with wild rice or boiled rice and a tossed salad.

Quail with white grapes

6 servings

- *6 quail*
- *6 slices bacon*
- *2 onions, thinly sliced*
- *2 carrots, finely chopped*
- *$^1/_2$ cup white wine*
- *1 cup seedless white grapes*

Cumberland sauce:
- *1 orange*
- *1 lemon*
- *3 scallions, finely chopped*
- *1 cup water*
- *$^1/_3$ cup port wine*
- *4 tablespoons red currant jelly*
- *1 teaspoon prepared mild mustard*
- *$^1/_8$ teaspoon ginger powder*

Wrap each quail with a bacon strip. Place the sliced onions and carrots in a large baking dish. Place the quail on the bed of vegetables. Add the white wine. Roast the quail uncovered in a preheated 450° oven for 25 minutes. Discard the bacon and continue cooking for 10 minutes until the quail are lightly browned and tender. Plunge the grapes into 1 cup of boiling water for 5 minutes. Drain the grapes. Arrange the quail on rounds of bread fried in butter. Garnish with hot white grapes and watercress. Serve with a Cumberland sauce. To prepare the Cumberland sauce, peel the orange and lemon rinds, cutting as closely to the colored part of the rind as possible. Chop the rind into tiny pieces about the size of a tomato seed. Simmer the fruit rinds and scallions in boiling water for 10 minutes. Drain through a fine strainer. Place the port wine, $^1/_2$ cup orange juice and red currant jelly in a small saucepan. Place over low heat. When the jelly has melted add the mustard and fruit rinds. Simmer 5 minutes. Stir in the ginger powder. Serve cold with hot quail, ham or cold meat.

Long Island duckling with peaches

4 servings

- *1 (4 pound) duckling*
- *3 tablespoons butter, softened*
- *3 tablespoons honey*
- *2 cups water*
- *1 cup sugar*
- *4 peaches*
- *1 bunch watercress*

Walnut dressing:
- *2 tablespoons butter*
- *1 cup chopped English walnuts*
- *2 onions, finely chopped*
- *3 cups freshly made breadcrumbs*
- *Grated rind of 1 lemon*
- *$^1/_2$ teaspoon cinnamon*
- *1 teaspoon sage*
- *$^1/_2$ teaspoon salt*
- *Freshly ground black pepper*
- *2 eggs, lightly beaten*

First prepare the dressing: Heat the butter in a skillet. Add the nuts and fry for 3 minutes over moderately high heat. Add the onions and continue cooking for 3 minutes. Remove from the heat and stir in the remaining ingredients.

Wash and dry the cavity of the duckling and add the dressing. Truss the duck or secure with poultry lacers. Place the duck on a rack in a roasting pan. Prick the duck skin all over with a fork. Combine the butter and honey in a custard cup and spread over the duck skin. Roast the duck, uncovered, in a preheated 350° oven for $1^1/_2$ hours.

To prepare the peaches: Pour the water into a saucepan. Add the sugar and boil for 2 minutes. Lower the heat and add the peaches. Simmer the peaches for 10 minutes until tender but not too soft. Drain the peaches. Garnish the duck with hot poached peaches and watercress. Carve the duck at the table or cut it into quarters with poultry shears.

The duck can be made completely in advance and served cold for a summer party. The texture of this dressing is very good and can also be used for stuffing a fine plump chicken. Leftover dressing can be frozen or used in duck or chicken sandwiches.

Long Island duckling stuffed with breadcrumbs and walnuts. The honeyed skin is sweet and crisp (recipe page 31, 3rd column).

Chicken dishes

There are as many ways of cooking Southern fried chicken as there are states in the union. This batter is light and full of flavor. It is equally good served hot or cold.

Southern fried chicken

6 servings

2 (3 pound) frying chickens, cut into serving pieces
³/₄ cup flour
¹/₄ teaspoon salt
1 cup milk
1 egg
2 tablespoons vegetable oil
Oil or shortening for deep frying

Combine the flour, salt, milk, egg and vegetable oil in a bowl. Stir with a wire whisk to form a smooth batter. Dip the chicken pieces in the batter and fry in hot oil for 30 minutes or until almost tender. Remove and drain the chicken on paper towels. Increase the heat under the oil and fry the chicken for 5 more minutes until the batter is crisp and golden.
Sometimes the fried chicken is drizzled with liquid honey just before serving. Serve the chicken in a wicker basket with French fries and hot bread or corn bread.

Chicken salad

4 servings

- 2 cups cooked chicken
- 1 cup boiled ham
- 2 stalks celery, sliced
- 1 cup mayonnaise
- 1 teaspoon prepared mustard
- 1 teaspoon lemon juice
- 4 small potatoes, boiled
- 1 head Boston lettuce
- 2 tomatoes, sliced
- 1 cucumber, sliced
- 1 avocado, sliced

Cut the chicken and ham into man sized cubes. Simmer the celery in salted water for 5 minutes. Drain and rinse under cold water.
Combine the mayonnaise, mustard and lemon juice. Fold the dressing into the chicken, ham, celery and potatoes. Line a salad bowl with lettuce leaves. Arrange the chicken salad on the lettuce and garnish with alternating slices of tomato, cucumber and avocado.

Chicken breasts with ham and cheese

4 servings

- 8 chicken breasts
- 8 thin slices boiled ham
- 8 thin slices mozzarella cheese
- $1/2$ cup flour, seasoned with
- 1 teaspoon salt and Freshly ground black pepper
- 2 eggs, lightly beaten
- $3/4$ cup freshly made breadcrumbs
- 4 tablespoons butter
- 2 tablespoons oil

Ask the butcher to remove the skin and bones from the chicken breasts and pound them as thin as a veal scallopini. Place a slice of ham and cheese on each chicken breast and fold the breast over to make a sandwich. Trim any ham and cheese protruding from the edges and press slightly to seal in place. Dip each filled breast first in seasoned flour, then in beaten egg and finally in breadcrumbs. Divide the combined butter and oil between 2 large skillets. Heat until hot and fry the chicken breasts 10 minutes on each side until tender. Serve with rice and spinach.

Chicken in a pot

4 servings

- 1 (3 pound) frying chicken, cut into serving pieces
- 2 tablespoons butter
- 1 tablespoon oil
- 1 onion, finely chopped
- 1 green pepper, finely chopped
- 1 cup uncooked rice
- $2^{1}/2$ cups chicken broth
- 1 tablespoon tomato paste
- 1 teaspoon summer savory or
- $1/2$ teaspoon oregano
- $1/2$ teaspoon thyme
- $1/2$ teaspoon salt Freshly ground black pepper

Brown the chicken pieces in hot combined butter and oil. Remove the chicken and fry the onion and green pepper for 3 minutes. Place the rice in a 3 quart casserole. Spread the onion and green pepper over the rice. Arrange the chicken pieces over the vegetables. Add all the remaining ingredients. Cover and bake in a preheated 350° over for 50 minutes until the rice has absorbed all the liquid. Serve from the casserole.

Barbecued chicken

- 2 (2 to $2^{1}/2$ pound) broiling chickens, cut in half
- $1^{1}/2$ teaspoons salt Freshly ground black pepper
- $1/4$ pound butter Juice of 2 limes
- $1/4$ cup catsup Few drops Tabasco sauce
- $1/2$ teaspoon Worcestershire sauce
- 1 teaspoon savory
- 1 teaspoon thyme
- 1 clove garlic, crushed

Wash and dry the chickens thoroughly. Sprinkle on all sides with $1/2$ teaspoon salt and pepper. Melt the butter in a saucepan and add all the remaining ingredients, stirring to combine thoroughly. Brush the chickens with the sauce and place on an oiled rack, skin side up, over a hot charcoal fire. Grill about 20 minutes on each side, basting frequently with the sauce. You may also cook the chickens under a hot oven broiler for the same period of time.

This dish is often served at fund raising suppers and is traditionally served with corn bread. See recipe on page 80.

35

Chicken casserole with vegetables

4 servings

1 (3 pound) roasting chicken
2 tablespoons butter
1 tablespoon oil
2 onions, finely chopped
2 carrots, finely chopped
2 stalks celery, finely chopped
$^1/_2$ cup chicken broth
$^1/_2$ teaspoon salt
    Freshly ground black pepper
1 teaspoon marjoram
1 tablespoon cornstarch dissolved in 2 tablespoons cold water
2 tablespoons finely chopped parsley

Truss the chicken and brown it breast side first in hot combined butter and oil in a casserole. Remove the chicken. Fry the vegetables in the same butter and oil for 3 minutes until softened. Replace the chicken on the bed of vegetables. Add the chicken broth, salt, pepper and marjoram. Cover and bake in a preheated 350° oven for 50 minutes. Remove the chicken and cut it into serving pieces. Stir the cornstarch paste into the broth and stir with a wire whisk until thickened into a medium thick sauce. Replace the chicken pieces. Garnish with parsley. Serve from the casserole with rice.

Chicken with red wine

6 servings

4 slices bacon, diced
2 (2$^1/_2$ pound) frying chickens, cut into serving pieces
1 medium sized onion, finely chopped
2 cloves garlic, crushed
2 tablespoons brandy, heated
1$^1/_2$ cups red wine
$^1/_2$ cup chicken broth
$^1/_2$ teaspoon salt
    Freshly ground black pepper
1 bay leaf
$^1/_2$ teaspoon thyme
1 tablespoon tomato paste
6 carrots, peeled and cut into strips
$^1/_2$ pound mushrooms, left whole if small and quartered if large
3 tablespoons flour combined with 1$^1/_2$ tablespoons softened butter

Fry the bacon in a heavy casserole until crisp. Remove bacon from the pan. Sauté the chicken, onion and garlic in the rendered bacon fat. Light the brandy and pour the flames over the chicken. Add the wine, broth, salt, pepper, bay leaf, thyme, tomato paste and carrots. Bring to a simmer, cover and cook slowly 30 minutes. Add mushrooms, cover and simmer 15 minutes more. Remove bay leaf.
With a wire whisk, stir flour/butter mixture into liquid by bits and simmer until thickened. Serve from the casserole.

Brunswick stew

6 servings

3 strips bacon, cut into small pieces
1 (5 pound) stewing hen or 2 (2$^1/_2$ pound) stewing chickens
2 onions, finely chopped
3 carrots, chopped
3 stalks celery, chopped
2 tablespoons flour
2$^1/_2$ cups chicken broth
2 bay leaves
1 (10 ounce) package frozen lima beans
1 (12 ounce) can corn niblets
3 tomatoes, peeled, seeded and chopped
1 teaspoon salt
    Freshly ground black pepper

Fry the bacon until the fat is rendered. Remove the bacon and place in a casserole. Brown the chicken in hot bacon fat and place in the casserole. Fry the onions, carrots and celery for 5 minutes until softened. Add the flour and cook 1 minute. Stir in $^1/_2$ cup of the chicken broth. Transfer all these ingredients to the casserole. Add the remaining chicken broth and bay leaves. Cover and bake in a preheated 350° oven for 1$^3/_4$ hours for the 5 pound hen and 1 hour for the 2$^1/_2$ pound chickens. Remove the chicken from the bones and cut into small pieces. Return the chicken to the casserole and add the lima beans, corn, tomatoes, salt and pepper to the casserole. Simmer for 10 minutes. Discard the bay leaves and serve in soup bowls.

Broiled chicken with mustard

4 servings

1 (3 pound) frying chicken, cut into serving pieces
5 tablespoons butter
2 teaspoons prepared mild mustard
1 teaspoon Worcestershire sauce
1 teaspoon rosemary
2 tablespoons finely chopped parsley
$^1/_2$ teaspoon salt
    Freshly ground black pepper

Place the chicken pieces in a buttered baking dish and dot with 2 tablespoons of butter. Bake in a preheated 400° oven for 20 minutes. Combine the remaining butter with mustard, Worcestershire sauce, rosemary, parsley, salt and pepper. Brush half the mixture over the chicken pieces. Place under a preheated broiler for 12 minutes. Turn the chicken and brush with the remaining butter mixture. Broil for 12 to 15 minutes until the chicken is tender.

Chicken Pot Pie is a favorite with everybody in the family. To be absolutely authentic to its British origin, substitute the biscuits for four and twenty blackbirds.

Chicken pot pie

6 servings

     1 *(4 pound) stewing chicken, quartered*
     1 *onion, sliced*
     1 *carrot, peeled and sliced*
     1 *stalk celery, sliced*
     8 *peppercorns*
     1 *bay leaf*
     4 *parsley stems*
  $^1/_2$ *teaspoon thyme*
     4 *tablespoons butter*
     1 *onion, finely chopped*
     6 *tablespoons flour*
     1 *teaspoon paprika*
     2 *cups reserved chicken broth*
  $^1/_3$ *cup dry white wine*
        Juice of 1 lemon
     1 *teaspoon salt*
        Freshly ground black pepper
     2 *tablespoons finely chopped parsley*
     1 *(15 ounce) can baby carrots, drained*
     1 *(10 ounce) package frozen tiny peas, thawed*
     1 *recipe biscuits (recipe page 78, 3rd column)*

Place the chicken, onion, carrot, celery, peppercorns, bay leaf, parsley stems and thyme in a casserole. Add water to cover the ingredients and bring to a boil. Lower the heat, cover and simmer 1 hour or until the chicken is tender. Remove the chicken from the broth and set aside to cool. Strain the broth and chill until the fat rises to the surface. Discard the skin and bones of the chicken and cut the meat into strips. Skim the fat from the broth and measure 2

Chicken with tomatoes is at its best in the summer when fresh tomatoes are bursting with ripeness and flavor.

Chicken with tomatoes

Lemon chicken with herbs

cups. Melt the butter. Add the chopped onion and sauté until softened. Add the flour and paprika and cook, stirring, 2 minutes. Add the chicken broth gradually, stirring constantly until the sauce thickens. Add the wine, lemon juice, salt, pepper and parsley and simmer 5 minutes. Add the reserved chicken, carrots and peas to the sauce and combine gently but thoroughly. Spoon the mixture into a 2 quart ovenproof serving dish. Prepare the biscuit mixture as directed on page 78. Roll out and cut the biscuits. Cover mixture with biscuits, bake, uncovered, in a 450° oven 20 minutes.

6 servings

   2 *(2^1/$_2$ pound) frying chickens,*
     cut into serving pieces
   2 *tablespoons butter*
   1 *tablespoon oil*
   1 *onion, finely chopped*
   1 *clove garlic, crushed*
   4 *medium sized tomatoes,*
     peeled, seeded and chopped
   1 *tablespoon tomato paste*
^{1}/$_4$ *cup tomato purée*
   3 *bay leaves*
^{1}/$_2$ *teaspoon basil*
   1 *cup white wine*
^{1}/$_2$ *cup chicken broth*
   1 *teaspoon salt*
    Freshly ground black pepper

   1 *tablespoon cornstarch*
    dissolved in
   2 *tablespoons cold water*
   2 *tablespoons finely chopped*
    parsley

Brown chicken in hot combined butter and oil. Remove the chicken from the skillet. Fry the onion and garlic in the same butter for 3 minutes. Replace the chicken pieces in the pan. Add ^{1}/$_2$ the tomato pieces and all the remaining ingredients except the cornstarch and parsley. Cover and simmer for 40 minutes. Remove the chicken pieces and keep them hot. Strain the juice into a saucepan. Return the sauce to simmering point and stir in the remaining tomatoes and the cornstarch paste. Arrange the chicken in a serving dish and spoon the sauce over each piece. Garnish with parsley. This is a particularly good chicken dish, especially when the tomatoes are in season. It can be served with plain or saffron rice.

6 servings

   4 *tablespoons butter*
   2 *(2^1/$_2$ pound) frying chickens*
     cut into serving pieces
     Rind and juice of 2 lemons
^{1}/$_2$ *teaspoons salt*
    Freshly ground black
    pepper.
   1 *cup chicken broth*
   1 *tablespoon cornstarch*
    dissolved in
   2 *tablespoons cold water*
   1 *teaspoon paprika*
^{1}/$_2$ *teaspoon rosemary*
^{1}/$_2$ *teaspoon mint*
   1 *tablespoon finely*
    chopped parsley

Melt 2 tablespoons butter in a casserole. Add the chicken pieces, the pared rind of 2 lemons and the juice of 1 lemon. Season the chicken with salt and pepper. Cover and bake in a preheated 325° oven for 40 minutes. (Do not worry that there should be more liquid in the casserole.) Butter a baking dish and arrange the partially cooked chicken pieces in a single layer. Add the chicken broth to the strained juices from the casserole. Simmer for 5 minutes and stir in cornstarch dissolved in cold water. In the meantime squeeze the remaining lemon over the chicken. Dot the chicken with the remaining butter and sprinkle with the paprika and combined herbs. Broil the chicken until crisp and golden. Serve sauce separately.

Fish dishes

The shores, rivers and lakes of America teem with hundreds of varieties of fish, and the best are always the freshest. Choosing and cooking fish is largely a question of common sense – hence its claim to be 'brain food.' Only fish which looks appetizing, with a gleam in its eye and shine on its silvery skin, will taste good. Elderly fish tend to affect the stomach more than the brain.

Fish is so plentiful in America that it is always best to substitute a fresh, local variety than to search for the frozen specific called for in a particular recipe. Both salt and fresh water fish are interchangeable within their categories. They are described as being either fat or lean. Lean fish are generally fried, sautéed in butter, steamed or poached. In other words, they are cooked in liquid of some form or another and frequently served with buttery or creamy sauces. Fat fish are broiled or baked, using a dry method of cooking.

Deep sea game fishing is an immensely popular sport in America, though sometimes it is difficult to know whether the real game is the catch or the beer which is drunk to sustain the fishermen. Fishing is not just a summer pleasure. Even when the lakes are frozen, small holes are cut into the ice and hardy enthusiasts sit in tiny shelters, bundled in layers of clothing, with their lines sunk into icy water. They huddle, often for hours, in subzero temperatures for their unsuspecting supper to swim by and take the bait.

For those with less time, many states and private corporations have started fish hatcheries in which trout, salmon and shellfish are being bred, fed and protected until harvesting time.

Shrimp cocktail

6 servings

Sauce:
- 1 (16 ounce) can tomato purée
- 3/4 teaspoon salt
- 1/2 teaspoon dry mustard
- 1/2 tablespoon prepared horseradish
- 1/2 teaspoon Worcestershire sauce
  Few drops Tabasco sauce
- 2 teaspoons chopped capers
- 2 tablespoons finely chopped celery leaves
- 1 scallion, finely chopped

- 30 cooked jumbo shrimp
- 6 sprigs parsley

Combine all the sauce ingredients in a bowl and stir with a wire whisk until thoroughly combined. Cover and refrigerate several hours. Shell and devein the shrimp, but leave the tails intact. Chill until serving time. When ready to serve, place 1 tablespoon of sauce in each of 6 individual glass serving dishes. Arrange 5 shrimp in each dish, letting the tails swim over the edge. Top with more sauce and decorate with a parsley sprig.

Shrimp Creole

4 to 6 servings

- 4 tablespoons oil
- 2 onions, finely chopped
- 2 green peppers, finely chopped
- 2 stalks celery, finely chopped
- 1 clove garlic, crushed
- 2 (17 ounce) cans Italian style tomatoes
- 2 bay leaves
- 1 1/2 teaspoons salt
  Freshly ground black pepper
- 1/4 teaspoon cayenne pepper
  Juice of 1 lemon
- 1 teaspoon Worcestershire sauce
- 2 pounds shrimp, shelled and deveined

Heat the oil in a heavy casserole and sauté the onions, green peppers, celery and garlic 5 minutes. Add the tomatoes with their liquid, bay leaves, salt, pepper and cayenne pepper. Break up the tomatoes with the back of a fork. Cook the mixture, uncovered, at the barest possible simmer 30 minutes. Cover the pan and simmer 15 minutes more. Add the lemon juice, Worcestershire sauce and shrimp. Cover and cook 3 to 5 minutes or just until the shrimp turn pink. The length of time will depend on the size of the shrimp. Serve immediately over fluffy white rice.

Shrimp with herbs

4 servings

    2 pounds large fresh shrimp
    3 tablespoons butter
    4 scallions, finely chopped
    2 cloves garlic, crushed
    1 tablespoon lemon juice
 $^1/_4$ cup white wine
    1 tomato, peeled, seeded
       and chopped
    1 tablespoon finely chopped
       fresh basil or
    1 teaspoon dried basil
    3 tablespoons finely
       chopped parsley
 $^1/_2$ teaspoon salt
       Freshly ground black
       pepper

Shell and devein the shrimp.
Heat the butter in a large skillet
and sauté the shrimp over high
heat for 5 minutes until rosy
pink. Remove the shrimp and
keep them warm. Add scallions
and garlic to the same butter and
fry for 4 minutes. Add lemon
juice, wine, tomato, basil and
half of the parsley. Simmer 3
minutes until the tomato has
softened slightly. Return the
shrimp to the skillet. Season with
salt and pepper. Cook over high
heat until the shrimps are hot.
Garnish with remaining parsley
and serve on a bed of saffron or
white rice.
When a girl offers a bouquet of
basil to her boyfriend, she is
offering more than her
friendship.

Shad roe with bacon and eggs

4 servings

    4 tablespoons butter
    4 scallions, white and green
       part finely chopped
    4 shad roes (2 pair)
       Juice of 1 lemon
 $^1/_2$ cup white wine
 $^1/_3$ cup heavy cream
 $^1/_2$ teaspoon salt
    2 teaspoons cornstarch
       dissolved in
    2 tablespoons cold water
    4 eggs
   12 strips bacon

Heat 2 tablespoons of butter in a
large skillet. Add the scallions
and fry for 3 minutes until
softened. Add the shad roes and
cook 5 minutes on each side.
Remove the roes and keep them
warm. Add the lemon juice, wine
and heavy cream. Boil over high
heat for 3 minutes and stir in the
salt and cornstarch paste to
form a sauce.
Arrange the roes on a hot serving
dish and spoon the sauce over the
fish. In the meantime, fry the
eggs in the remaining butter and
cook the bacon until crisp. Serve
for brunch with hot rolls or
buttered toast.

Poached salmon steaks with dill sauce

4 servings

 $^1/_2$ onion, thinly sliced
    4 ($^1/_2$ pound) salmon steaks
       Water to cover the salmon
    1 teaspoon peppercorns
    1 bay leaf
    1 teaspoon salt
 $^1/_2$ lemon

Dill sauce:
    1 cup sour cream
       Juice of $^1/_2$ lemon
    2 scallions, finely chopped
 $^1/_2$ teaspoon dill weed

Place the onion slices in a large
skillet or fish poacher. Cover
with salmon steaks and add
water to cover the salmon. Add
peppercorns, bay leaf and salt.
Squeeze the lemon juice into the
pan and add the squeezed lemon
half. Simmer, uncovered, with
the water barely bubbling. Lift
the salmon steaks carefully from
the water and drain on a wire
rack.
To prepare the sauce, combine
all the sauce ingredients in a
small saucepan. Heat until just
warm.
Serve the salmon and the sauce
separately with boiled potatoes
and freshly shelled peas.

Baked trout

4 servings

    4 ($^3/_4$ pound) whole cleaned
       trout
    3 tablespoons butter,
       softened
    3 tablespoons finely
       chopped parsley
    2 tablespoons chopped
       chives
    2 teaspoons mild prepared
       mustard
    1 tablespoon lemon juice
 $^1/_3$ cup slivered almonds
    1 lemon cut into wedges
    4 sprigs parsley

Place the trout in a buttered
baking dish. Combine the butter,
parsley, chives, mustard and
lemon juice. Dot the mixture
over the fish. Cover with
aluminium foil and bake in a
preheated 350° oven for 10
minutes.
Discard the foil and scatter the
almonds over the trout. Bake
uncovered for 5 minutes until the
almonds are crisp and brown and
the fish is tender. Garnish the
dish with lemon wedges and
parsley sprigs.

For the stuffed lobster recipe:
Lobster is tied onto a wooden
board so its tail won't curl.

A piece is cut out of the back and
the meat removed to prepare it
for stuffing. (See recipe on page
41.)

Flounder with tartar sauce

6 servings

>   2 pounds flounder fillets
> ¹/₂ cup flour seasoned with
>   1 teaspoon salt and
>   Freshly ground black
>   pepper
>   2 eggs, lightly beaten
> ¹/₂ cup bread crumbs
>   Oil or shortening for
>   deep frying

Tartar sauce:

> ¹/₂ cup mayonnaise
>   1 clove garlic, crushed
>   1 teaspoon capers
>   1 tablespoon finely
>   chopped parsley
>   2 sweet gherkins, finely
>   chopped
>   1 teaspoon lemon juice

Dip the flounder in seasoned
flour, then into beaten egg and
finally into breadcrumbs. Fry in
deep hot fat a few pieces at a time
for 6 minutes. Drain on paper
towels and heat the cooking oil
until very hot. Fry the fish a
second time for 2 minutes until
brown and crisp. Drain and serve
immediately with tartar sauce
and French fried potatoes.
To prepare the sauce, combine
all the sauce ingredients in a
small bowl.

The boiled lobster meat is combined with a rich cream sauce and topped with cheese and breadcrumbs. You can place this stuffed lobster under the broiler for a moment to give it a final touch of color.

Stuffed lobster

4 servings

2 (2 pound) live lobsters
4 cups water
1 cup white wine
$^1/_4$ cup white vermouth
1 small onion, finely chopped
1 carrot, finely chopped
1 stalk celery, finely chopped
1 bay leaf
1 teaspoon salt
4 tablespoons butter
2 tablespoons flour
1 teaspoon tomato paste
2 egg yolks
$^1/_3$ cup heavy cream
$^1/_2$ cup breadcrumbs
$^1/_2$ cup grated Parmesan cheese

Tie the lobsters onto a wooden board so the tails will not curl. Place the water, wine, vermouth, onion, carrot, celery, bay leaf and salt in a small fish poacher or large saucepan. Bring to simmering point. Add the lobsters. Cook 1 at a time if the pan will not accomodate both. Cover and simmer for 18 minutes. Drain the lobsters. Remove the lobster meat and cut into bite sized pieces. Reserve the shells and cut a small opening in the back of the shell with a pair of scissors. Boil the poaching liquid until only $1^1/_2$ cups remain. Strain the liquid. Melt 2 tablespoons of the butter in a small saucepan. Stir in the flour and add the strained poaching liquid to form a smooth sauce. Stir in the tomato paste. Combine the egg yolks and cream. Remove the sauce from the heat and add the egg-yolk mixture and lobster. Replace in the lobster shells. Scatter with breadcrumbs and cheese and dot with remaining butter. Place under the broiler for 4 minutes until the sauce is bubbling and the crumbs are lightly browned. Arrange on a serving dish, shell side up. Serve $^1/_2$ lobster for each person. Garnish with parsley and lemon wedges.

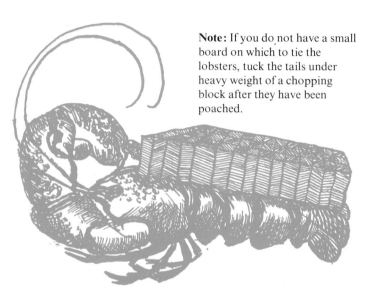

Note: If you do not have a small board on which to tie the lobsters, tuck the tails under heavy weight of a chopping block after they have been poached.

Oysters Rockefeller

4 servings

24 oysters
2 (10 ounce) packages frozen
  chopped spinach, cooked
  and thoroughly drained
4 scallions, finely chopped
6 tablespoons finely chopped
  parsley
$^1/_2$ cup fine dry breadcrumbs
$^1/_2$ teaspoon salt
  Freshly ground black
  pepper
$^1/_8$ teaspoon cayenne pepper
$^1/_2$ cup melted butter

Have the fishman open the
oysters. Loosen each oyster from
the shell and remove. Scrub the
shells and dry thoroughly.
Return the oysters to their shells
and arrange them in a baking
pan which has been lined with
rock salt. Combine all the
remaining ingredients in a
mixing bowl. Spread a spoonful
of the spinach mixture over each
oyster. Bake, uncovered, in a
preheated 450° oven 7 to 10
minutes. Transfer to individual
plates and serve immediately.

Scallops
with tomatoes

4 servings

2 pounds bay scallops
  or sea scallops
$^1/_2$ cup water
$^1/_2$ cup white wine
1 tablespoon lemon juice
1 bay leaf
4 scallions, finely chopped
1 teaspoon peppercorns
2 sprigs parsley
$^1/_2$ teaspoon salt
3 tablespoons butter
3 tablespoons flour
$^3/_4$ cup light cream
2 tomatoes, peeled, seeded
  and chopped
2 egg yolks
2 tablespoons finely
  chopped parsley

Wash the scallops. Place in a
saucepan and add the water,
wine and lemon juice. Tie the bay
leaf, scallions, peppercorns and
parsley into a piece of
cheesecloth and bury the bag
among the scallops. Season with
salt. Cover and simmer over low
heat for 8 minutes until the
scallops are white and almost
tender. Drain the scallops and, if
sea scallops are used, cut them
into small pieces. Discard the
cheesecloth bag and reserve the
cooking liquid.
Heat the butter in a clean
saucepan. Stir in the flour and
add $^1/_2$ cup cream and the
reserved cooking liquid
gradually. Stir with a wire whisk
to form a smooth sauce. Stir in
the tomatoes and scallops.
Combine the egg yolks with the
remaining cream and stir into the
sauce. Garnish with parsley and
serve on a bed of rice.

Maryland
steamed crabs

4 servings

2 cups vinegar
2 cups water
12 hard shelled live crabs
1 tablespoon dry mustard
1 teaspoon hot red pepper
  flakes

Pour the vinegar and water into a
large steamer. Place the crabs on
a rack and sprinkle each shell
with mustard powder and pepper
flakes. Cover the steamer with a
tight fitting lid and steam over
moderate heat for 15 minutes
until the shells turn bright red.
Serve with plenty of foaming ice
cold beer.

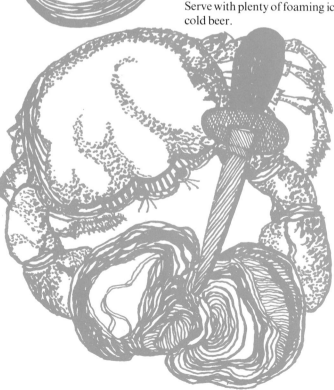

Baked clams

4 to 6 servings

      24 *cherrystone clams*
 1¹/₃ *cups fine dry breadcrumbs*
       2 *teaspoons oregano*
       2 *tablespoons finely chopped*
           parsley
       1 *teaspoon salt*
           Freshly ground black
           pepper
       4 *tablespoons grated*
           Parmesan cheese
       2 *tablespoons lemon juice*
       6 *tablespoons melted butter*

Scrub the clams well with a stiff brush. Open them with a clam opener or sharp knife. Loosen the clams from the shell and discard ¹/₂ of each shell. Sprinkle a baking pan or 4 individual gratin dishes with a ¹/₂ inch thick layer of rock salt. Arrange the clams on the half shell on the rock salt. Combine all the remaining ingredients in a bowl and mix thoroughly. Cover each clam completely with some of the breadcrumb mixture. Bake, uncovered, in a preheated 450° oven 10 minutes until the crumbs are golden brown. Serve immediately.

Fried clams with fruit sauce

4 servings

       2 *(7 ounce) cans minced*
           clams, drained or
      24 *steamer clams*
 1¹/₄ *cups flour*
       1 *teaspoon baking powder*
       1 *teaspoon paprika*
   ¹/₂ *teaspoon salt*
           Freshly ground black
           pepper
   ¹/₂ *cup beer*
   ¹/₂ *cup clam juice*
       1 *tablespoon lemon juice*
       1 *tablespoon oil*
           Oil or shortening for
           deep frying
           Parsley for garnish
       1 *lemon, cut into wedges*

Fruit sauce :

   ³/₄ *cup orange marmalade*
       4 *tablespoons lemon juice*
       2 *tablespoons orange juice*
       1 *tablespoon prepared*
           horseradish
   ¹/₂ *teaspoon powdered*
           ginger
   ¹/₂ *teaspoon dry mustard*
   ¹/₂ *teaspoon salt*

Soak fresh clams in a large bowl of cold water for 30 minutes to remove the sand. Steam the clams over 1 cup simmering water for 10 minutes until the shells open. Chop the clams finely or use drained canned clams.
Make a batter by combining the flour, baking powder, paprika, salt, pepper, beer, clam juice, lemon juice and 1 tablespoon of oil in a bowl. Add the clams.

Drop by tablespoons into deep hot fat and fry for 4 minutes until the batter is crisp and golden. Drain the clams.
In the meantime place all the ingredients for the sauce in a blender. Blend until smooth. Arrange the fried clam cakes on a hot serving dish. Garnish with parsley and lemon wedges and serve the sauce separately.

Halibut in cheese sauce

6 servings

       3 *pounds halibut cut*
           into 6 steaks
           Water
       1 *teaspoon salt*
       3 *tablespoons butter*
       6 *mushroom caps*
       2 *tablespoons flour*
 1³/₄ *cups milk*
   ¹/₂ *cup grated Gruyère*
           or Swiss cheese
       3 *tablespoons grated*
           Parmesan cheese
           Dash of cayenne pepper

Place the halibut in a large skillet. Cover with water and add salt. Simmer, uncovered, for 12 minutes until the fish is white and opaque and flakes easily. Remove and drain the fish. In the meantime, prepare the sauce. Heat the butter in a small saucepan and fry the mushrooms until lightly browned. Remove the mushrooms and wrap in foil to keep them warm. Stir the flour into the butter and add the milk gradually. Stir in the cheeses and cayenne pepper. Spoon the hot cheese sauce over the fish. Garnish with mushroom caps and serve immediately.

A whole red snapper is both beautiful and dramatic. The fish is stuffed with savory croutons, herbs and tomatoes.

Stuffed red snapper

6 servings

- 1 (5 pound) red snapper
- 2 tablespoons softened butter
- 1 teaspoon salt
  Freshly ground black pepper
  Juice of $^{1}/_{2}$ lemon
- 2 cups dry white wine

Stuffing:

- 4 slices bacon
- 1 medium sized onion, finely chopped
- $3^{1}/_{2}$ cups crisp croutons
- 1 teaspoon savory
- 1 teaspoon thyme
- 2 tablespoons finely chopped parsley
- 2 tablespoons finely chopped celery leaves
- $^{1}/_{2}$ teaspoon salt
  Freshly ground black pepper
- 1 egg, lightly beaten
  Juice of 1 lemon
- $^{1}/_{4}$ cup dry vermouth

Have the fishman remove the bones from the red snapper, but leave the head and tail intact. Rub the inside of the fish with 1 tablespoon butter and sprinkle with $^{1}/_{2}$ teaspoon salt and pepper. To prepare the stuffing, fry the bacon until crisp. Remove from the pan and drain on paper towels. Cook the onion in the rendered bacon fat until soft. Place the croutons in a mixing bowl. Crumble the bacon and add to the croutons. Add the onion with the bacon fat and all the remaining stuffing ingredients. Combine thoroughly. Stuff the fish with the mixture and sew up the opening with string or secure with skewers. Place the fish in a large buttered roasting tin. Rub with the remaining butter and sprinkle with the remaining salt, pepper and lemon juice. Pour the wine into the pan and bake the fish in a 400° oven 35 minutes or until the flesh flakes easily with a fork. Carefully transfer to a serving platter and remove the trussing strings or skewers. Surround the fish with sautéed fresh mushrooms and baby peas.

Salads

Caesar Salad is tossed at the last minute and served as a complete lunch or as an accompaniment to a succulent steak for dinner. Men love it.

Caesar salad

4 servings

1 large head Romaine lettuce

Dressing:
2 tablespoons vinegar
6 tablespoons oil
1/2 teaspoon salt
Freshly ground black pepper
1 teaspoon prepared mild mustard
2 cloves garlic, crushed
1 raw egg
2 tablespoons finely chopped parsley

1/2 pound bacon, fried until crisp

2 slices firm textured bread
2 tablespoons butter
1 tablespoon oil
2 hard boiled eggs, cut into wedges
6 fillets of anchovy
1/4 cup freshly grated Parmesan cheese

Cut the lettuce into bite sized pieces. Wash carefully to remove any sand and dry thoroughly. Combine all the ingredients for the dressing. Crumble the fried bacon into small pieces. Cut the bread into croutons and sauté the croutons in combined hot butter and oil until crisp and golden brown. Drain the croutons on paper towels. To assemble the salad, toss the lettuce with the dressing in a salad bowl. Scatter the crisp bacon over the lettuce. Arrange the wedges of hard boiled eggs around the edges of the bowl. Garnish the eggs with anchovies. Sprinkle the salad with Parmesan cheese.

Note: All the ingredients can be prepared in advance and the salad assembled at the last moment. Serve the salad as a luncheon dish or as an accompaniment to a broiled steak.

Cold duck salad

4 servings

     1   *(4 pound) duck*
     3   *stalks celery, chopped*
     2   *oranges*

Dressing:

     2   *tablespoons wine vinegar*
     6   *tablespoons salad oil*
   $^1/_2$ *teaspoon salt*
   $^1/_2$ *teaspoon prepared mild
          mustard*

Garnish:

     1   *head Boston lettuce*
    12   *black olives, pitted*
   $^1/_2$ *cup chopped English
          walnuts,*

Prick the duck skin with a fork.
Place on a rack in a roasting tin
and roast, uncovered, in a
preheated 350° oven for 1$^1/_2$
hours until tender. Discard the
skin and bones and cut the duck
into bite sized pieces. Combine
the duck and celery. Grate and
reserve the rind of 1 orange.
Peel the white pith from the
oranges and cut into segments,
cutting between the membranes.
Combine the orange segments
with the duck and celery.
Combine the dressing
ingredients, adding the reserved
grated orange rind. Toss with the
duck. Line a glass salad bowl
with lettuce leaves. Arrange the
duck over the lettuce and garnish
with olives. Sprinkle the duck
mixture with chopped nuts.
Serve with crusty bread.

Cole slaw

4 servings

     3   *cups crisp shredded cabbage*
   $^1/_2$ *cup coarsely grated carrot*
   $^1/_4$ *cup finely sliced scallion*
     2   *tablespoons chopped
          parsley*

Dressing:

     2   *tablespoons flour*
   1$^1/_2$ *teaspoons salt*
   $^3/_4$ *teaspoon dry mustard*
     2   *teaspoons sugar
          Freshly ground black
          pepper*
     1   *egg, beaten*
     1   *cup milk*
     4   *tablespoons vinegar*
     2   *tablespoons butter*

Shred the cabbage finely and mix
in a salad bowl with the carrot,
scallion and parsley.
Dressing: Mix the flour, salt,
mustard, sugar and pepper. Add
the egg and milk. Cook in a
double boiler over hot water
until thick, stirring constantly.
Remove from heat, add the
vinegar and butter, cover and
refrigerate. Combine the chilled
dressing with the cabbage
mixture.

Lobster salad

6 servings

     2   *(3 pound) live lobsters*
     1   *head Boston lettuce*
     3   *hard boiled eggs, sliced*
     3   *small tomatoes, sliced*
     1   *cucumber, sliced*
    18   *black olives, pitted*
     1   *lemon, cut into wedges*

Place the lobsters in a large pot of
simmering salted water. Cover
and boil gently for 20 minutes.
Drain and cool the lobsters.
Remove the lobster meat and cut
into neat bite-sized pieces.
Arrange the lettuce leaves on a
serving plate. Place the lobster
pieces in the center of the leaves.
Arrange alternating slices of
hard-boiled egg, tomato and
cucumber around the plate.
Garnish with black olives and
lemon wedges. Serve with
mayonnaise.
If you discover that you have a
lady lobster, reserve the coral
and stir it into the mayonnaise.

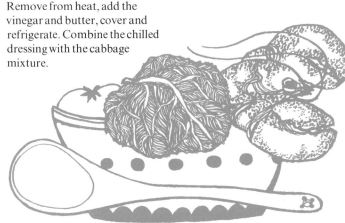

Chef's salad

6 servings

     2   *heads Romaine lettuce*
     1   *cup cold chicken,
          cut into man sized chunks*
   $^1/_2$ *cup cold tongue,
          cut into strips*
   $^1/_2$ *cup boiled ham,
          cut into strips*
   $^1/_2$ *cup Swiss cheese,
          cut into strips*
     3   *hard boiled eggs,
          cut in wedges*

Dressing:

     2   *tablespoons vinegar*
     6   *tablespoons salad oil*
     1   *clove garlic, crushed*
   $^1/_2$ *teaspoon salt
          Freshly ground black
          pepper*
     2   *tablespoons finely chopped
          parsley*
     4   *scallions, finely chopped*

Cut the lettuce into bite sized
pieces. Wash and dry
thoroughly. Divide the lettuce
between 6 individual salad
bowls. Place part of the chicken
in the center of each bowl.
Arrange the tongue, ham and
cheese strips like spokes of a
wheel around the bowl. Arrange
the egg wedges around the
chicken. Combine the
ingredients for the dressing in a
bowl and serve the dressing
separately.
The ingredients for a chef's salad
can be varied endlessly, adding
olives, tuna fish, sardines, chick
peas or any delights which the
chef has secreted in the refrigerator

Spinach salad

6 servings

- 1 pound fresh spinach
- 6 strips bacon, fried until crisp and crumbled
- 6 scallions, thinly sliced
- 1/4 pound raw mushrooms, thinly sliced

Dressing:

- 2 tablespoons lemon juice
- 6 tablespoons olive oil
- 1 clove garlic, crushed
- 1/2 teaspoon salt
  Freshly ground black pepper
- 1/8 teaspoon dry mustard
- 1/4 teaspoon sugar
- 1 egg yolk

Remove the tough stalks from the spinach, tear the leaves into bite sized pieces and place in a salad bowl. Toss in the bacon, scallions and mushrooms. Combine the ingredients for the dressing in a small jar. Cover tightly and shake vigorously to blend.
Just before serving pour about 1/2 to 3/4 of the dressing over the spinach and toss thoroughly.

Waldorf salad

4 servings

- 3 to 4 tart red apples
- 2 teaspoons sugar
  Juice of 1/2 lemon
- 2 stalks celery, finely chopped
- 3/4 cup coarsely chopped walnuts or pecans
- 1/4 cup mayonaise
- 1/4 cup heavy cream, whipped
- 4 lettuce leaves

Core and dice the apples, leaving the peel on 1 or 2 for color. Toss with the sugar and lemon juice. Add the celery and nuts and mix carefully with a wooden spoon. Fold the mayonnaise and whipped cream together, add to the apple mixture and toss thoroughly. Place the lettuce leaves on individual plates and mound the salad in the center. Chill 1 hour before serving.

Macaroni salad

4 to 6 servings

- 1/2 pound macaroni, broken into small pieces
- 1/4 cup undiluted evaporated milk
- 1 tablespoon vinegar
- 1 green pepper, finely chopped
- 1 stalk celery, finely chopped
- 4 scallions, finely chopped
- 2 canned pimientos, finely chopped
- 1/4 cup finely chopped black olives
- 1/4 cup finely chopped parsley
- 1/4 cup mayonnaise
- 1/2 teaspoon salt
  Freshly ground black pepper

Cook the macaroni in plenty of boiling salted water about 15 minutes or until very tender. Drain. Combine the evaporated milk and vinegar in a small bowl and set aside. Place the macaroni in a bowl and add the green pepper, celery, scallions, pimientos, olives and parsley. Chill 1 hour. Stir the mayonnaise, salt and pepper into the evaporated milk. Toss the macaroni with the dressing and chill 1 hour more before serving.

Avocado and shrimp salad

6 servings

- 1 head Boston lettuce
- 2 (4 1/2 ounce) cans baby shrimp
- 2 ripe avocados

Wash and dry the lettuce thoroughly. Tear into pieces and place in a salad bowl. Drain and dry the shrimp thoroughly and add to the lettuce. Chill until ready to serve. Just before serving, peel the avocados, cut them into cubes and place in the salad bowl. Toss the salad with 1/3 to 1/2 cup salad dressing and serve immediately.

Dressing for avocado and shrimp salad:

- 1 clove garlic, crushed
- 3 tablespoons minced anchovies
- 3 tablespoons finely chopped chives or scallions
- 1 tablespoon lemon juice
- 3 tablespoons tarragon vinegar
- 1 teaspoon prepared (Dijon type) mustard
- 1/2 teaspoon Worcestershire sauce
- 1/2 cup heavy cream
- 1 cup mayonnaise
- 1/3 cup finely chopped parsley
  Freshly ground black pepper

Combine ingredients in the order listed. Chill thoroughly.

Tomato aspic is a sculpture...a shimmering complement to cold sliced beef or chicken.

Tomato aspic

6 servings

1 (2 pound) can tomatoes
1 teaspoon tomato paste
1 tablespoon lemon juice
³/₄ cup chicken broth
1 clove garlic, crushed
¹/₂ teaspoon thyme
¹/₂ teaspoon allspice
1 teaspoon basil
1 bay leaf
2 tablespoons sherry
2 packages unflavored
  gelatin

Place the tomatoes with their liquid in a saucepan. Stir in the tomato paste, lemon juice, ¹/₂ cup chicken broth, garlic, thyme, allspice, basil and bay leaf. Cover and simmer over low heat for 10 minutes and force the mixture through a fine strainer. Add the sherry. Pour the remaining ¹/₄ cup of chicken broth into a small saucepan.
Sprinkle the gelatin over the liquid (sprinkle any dry gelatin crystals with water to cover completely). Allow the gelatin to stand undisturbed for 3 minutes. Place over low heat and dissolve the gelatin. Stir the gelatin liquid into the hot tomato broth. Pour into a 4 cup mold. Chill in the refrigerator for 4 hours before serving. Serve with cold chicken or sliced cold meat and an arrangement of cold cooked vegetables.

Blue cheese salad dressing

1 cup mayonnaise
¹/₄ cup heavy cream
1 teaspoon mild mustard
1 clove
1 clove garlic, crushed
¹/₃ cup blue cheese
¹/₄ teaspoon sage
¹/₄ teaspoon thyme

Place all the ingredients in an electric mixer and beat until smooth. Serve with a tossed salad or as a dressing for a potato salad.
This excellent flavorful dressing will keep at least 2 weeks in the refrigerator. If it becomes too thick as it stands, thin it with more cream and a tablespoon or 2 of vinegar.

Russian dressing

1 cup mayonnaise
1 tablespoon chili sauce
1 teaspoon mild mustard
  Dash of Tabasco sauce
1 teaspoon Worcestershire
  sauce
¹/₂ teaspoon salt

Combine all the ingredients in a bowl and serve as a dressing with sliced tomatoes or shrimp salad. The Hindu recipe for Worcestershire sauce was brought to England by Sir Marcus Sandys, a former governor of Bengal. Having eaten the sauce for many years, he was anxious to share it with his friends and also have a supply for himself. He took the sauce to a local drug store in Worcestershire and there the shop owners, Mr. John Lea and Mr. William Perrins, not only recreated the recipe but soon expanded into larger quarters as the popularity of their concoction spread around the world.

Thousand island dressing

1 cup mayonnaise
1 (2 ounce) jar red caviar
1 hard boiled egg,
  finely chopped
3 black olives, finely chopped
3 green olives, finely chopped

Combine all the ingredients in a bowl and serve with a salad made with Romaine and Boston lettuce.
This dressing gets its name from the thousand tiny islands of color.

Egg dishes

Eggs Benedict

6 servings

- 6 eggs
- 1 teaspoon salt
- 1 teaspoon vinegar
- 6 slices Canadian bacon
- 3 English muffins, split in half
  Hollandaise sauce
  (recipe page 18)
- 6 thin slices black truffle
  (optional)
- 6 sprigs parsley

Break each egg into a plate or small shallow dish. Fill a large, wide mouthed pan with water and add salt and vinegar. Bring the water to a slow simmer. Stir the water with a spoon and carefully slip 1 egg into the center of the swirl. Continue until all the eggs are in the pan. Maintain the water at the barest possible simmer and poach the eggs 4 to 5 minutes until the whites are set. Transfer the eggs with a slotted spoon to a bowl of warm water. Sauté the Canadian bacon 2 to 3 minutes on each side. Toast the muffins. Place a slice of bacon on each muffin half and keep warm in a 200° oven.

Prepare the Hollandaise sauce as directed in recipe page 18. To assemble Eggs Benedict, place a muffin half on each of 6 individual serving plates. Drain the eggs on paper towels and place on top of the bacon. Spoon the sauce over the eggs and decorate with a slice of truffle, if desired. Garnish each serving with a parsley sprig and serve immediately.

Huevos rancheros

6 servings

- 4 tablespoons butter
- 1 onion, finely chopped
- 1 clove garlic, crushed
- 1 green pepper, finely chopped
- 1 pound ground beef
- 1 teaspoon chili powder
- 1 tomato, peeled, seeded and chopped
- 1 tablespoon flour
- 1/2 cup beef broth
- 1 teaspoon salt
  Freshly ground black pepper
- 6 eggs

Heat 2 tablespoons butter in a skillet. Fry the onion, garlic and green pepper for 3 minutes until softened. Add ground beef and cook until the beef is lightly browned. Pour off all the accumulated fat. Stir in the chili powder and tomato. Stir in the flour and add the beef broth, salt and pepper. Simmer for 10 minutes. Fry the eggs in the remaining butter. Place the eggs on top of the beef and serve with tortillas.

Eggs on corned beef hash

6 servings

- 2 tablespoons butter
- 1 medium sized onion, finely chopped
- 1 small green pepper, seeded and finely chopped
- 3 cups finely chopped leftover corned beef
- 2 cups diced boiled potatoes
- 2 teaspoons Worcestershire sauce
  Freshly ground black pepper
- 1/4 cup beef broth (approximately)
- 6 poached eggs (see recipe for Eggs Benedict on this page)

Heat the butter in a skillet and sauté the onion and green pepper until softened. Add the corned beef, potatoes, Worcestershire sauce and pepper and sauté 3 to 4 minutes. Add the broth 1 tablespoon at a time until the mixture just sticks together. Place a portion of the hash in each of 6 individual ramekins. Keep warm in a very low oven. Poach the eggs and top each serving of hash with an egg. Garnish with parsley and serve.

Vegetable dishes

Asparagus with ham

Spinach soufflé

With the exception of iceberg lettuce and pascal celery, almost all the world's vegetables have been known for hundreds and hundreds of years, and almost all of them were once wild plants. Generations of people have decided to eat only the leaves of the spinach plant and only the stalks of the asparagus. The flowers of cauliflower taste good, but not the roots, while the reverse is true of the potato and we only eat the part that grows beneath the ground.

Potatoes were viewed with a certain amount of suspicion at various times in their history, mainly because it was a long time before anybody discovered how to make them into flour for bread. Scottish fundamentalists denounced potatoes because they were not mentioned in the Bible, while at the same time the grandson of Frederic the Great in Germany threatened to cut off the nose of anybody who would not plant them. And Marie Antoinette danced lightheartedly through France with potato blossoms in her hair while the priests and altar boys walked in solemn procession through the potato fields of Ireland, sprinkling the plants with holy water and praying for Divine intervention to produce a bountiful crop for the hungry people.

Tomatoes, which grew in Mexico before the year 1 A.D., were not eaten in western Europe until the 16th century. Some said that tomatoes were poisonous because their blossoms resembled deadly nightshade. Others, however, were convinced that it was a small green tomato, known as the love apple, that tempted Adam in the Garden of Eden. (The love apple then blushed red with shame.) Even in America, tomatoes did not become popular until a young French painter who had settled in Rhode Island, called a gathering of his friends and neighbors and publicly ate one of the tomatoes growing in his flower garden. When it became clear that he was going to survive the daring feat, the news of the 'discovery' of the tomato spread across the land.

Asparagus with ham

6 servings

  2 pounds tender, young asparagus
12 thin slices boiled ham

For the Hollandaise sauce:
$^1/_2$ stick butter
  3 egg yolks
$^1/_4$ teaspoon salt
    Dash of cayenne pepper
  2 tablespoons lemon juice

Cut off the tough ends of the asparagus and peel each spear. Tie the spears together in 2 or 3 bundles, leaving 1 spear loose. Bring plenty of salted water to a boil. Add the asparagus and simmer about 8 minutes or until the stalks are just tender (use the loose spear to test for doneness). While the asparagus is cooking, arrange 2 slices of ham on each of 6 individual serving plates. Drain the asparagus when it is done and arrange the spears over the ham slices.

Melt the butter in a small saucepan. It should be hot but not bubbling. Place all the remaining ingredients in an electric blender and blend about 5 seconds. Turn the blender to the lowest speed and add the butter slowly in a continuous stream. Turn the water off as soon as all the butter has been added and is thoroughly combined. Spoon the sauce over the asparagus and serve immediately.

Spinach soufflé

6 servings

  1 pound fresh spinach or 1 (10 ounce) package frozen spinach
$^1/_4$ cup water
  3 tablespoons butter
  3 tablespoons flour
$^1/_2$ cup milk
  1 tablespoon minced onion
$^1/_2$ teaspoon salt
    Freshly ground black pepper
$^1/_4$ teaspoon nutmeg
  2 teaspoons horseradish
  1 teaspoon lemon juice
  3 eggs, separated

Cook the spinach in $^1/_4$ cup water, drain, chop finely and set aside. Melt the butter, stir in the flour and cook for 2 minutes. Gradually add the milk, stirring constantly. Add the onion, salt, pepper, nutmeg and horseradish. Bring to a boil and cook gently until the sauce thickens.

Add the lemon juice and remove from the heat. Add the beaten egg yolks and cool for 15 minutes. Stir in the well drained spinach. Beat the egg whites until stiff and gently fold into the spinach mixture. Pour into a 6 cup buttered soufflé dish and bake, uncovered, in a preheated 350° oven for 35 minutes.

Braised celery

6 servings

    3 bunches celery hearts or
      1 bunch celery
    1 cup boiling beef broth
    1 onion, finely chopped
    1 carrot, finely chopped
    1 teaspoon tomato paste
    2 strips bacon, cut into
      small pieces
    1 tablespoon cornstarch
      dissolved in
      2 tablespoons cold water
    2 tablespoons finely chopped
      parsley

Separate the celery stalks and wash carefully. Cut lengthwise into thin strips and then into 6 inch pieces. Place the celery in a saucepan. Cover with boiling water. Cover and simmer for 10 minutes. Drain the celery and place in a baking dish. Add the beef broth, onion, carrot, tomato paste and bacon. Cover and cook in a preheated 350° oven for 40 minutes until tender. Stir in the cornstarch paste and cook over low heat for 2 minutes until the liquid has thickened into a sauce. Garnish with chopped parsley. If your baking dish cannot be placed over direct heat, strain the juices into a saucepan and add the cornstarch paste. Spoon the completed sauce over the celery.

String beans

6 servings

    2 pounds tender green beans
    2 tablespoons butter
    1 scallion, finely chopped
  $^1/_2$ cup slivered almonds
      Juice of 1 lemon
  $^1/_2$ teaspoon salt
      Freshly ground black
      pepper

Wash and trim the beans. Cut them into 2 inch lengths. Cook the beans in plenty of boiling, salted water 10 minutes or until barely tender. Drain the beans. Just before serving, heat the butter in a skillet and sauté the scallion and almonds 3 minutes, stirring constantly. Add the lemon juice, salt, pepper and beans and toss the beans for 1 to 2 minutes until heated through. Transfer to a heated serving dish and serve immediately.

Stuffed green peppers

6 servings

    6 medium sized green peppers
    1 tablespoon butter
    1 small onion, chopped
    1 pound ground chuck steak
    1 teaspoon salt
      Freshly ground black
      pepper
    1 tablespoon chopped parsley
    1 teaspoon Worcestershire
      sauce
    1 cup cooked rice
  $1^1/_4$ cups prepared tomato sauce
    1 egg

Wash the peppers and cut off the stalk end. Remove the seeds and membranes and cook in boiling salted water for 8 minutes. Drain. Heat the butter in a frying pan, add the onion and fry for 5 minutes. Add the meat and fry gently for 10 minutes until browned. Mix in the salt, pepper, parsley, Worcestershire sauce and cooked rice. Beat $^1/_4$ cup of the tomato sauce with the egg and stir into the meat mixture. Fill the pepper shells with the meat mixture and place in a buttered baking dish. Pour 2 tablespoons tomato sauce over the top of each one and pour the remaining sauce into the dish. Bake in a preheated 375° oven for 25 minutes.

Cucumbers with peas and scallions

4 servings

    2 firm cucumbers
    1 cup peas
    1 bunch scallions, finely
      chopped
  $^1/_2$ teaspoon salt
  $^1/_2$ teaspoon sugar
    2 tablespoons butter
  $^1/_2$ cup sour cream
      Freshly ground black
      pepper

Peel the cucumbers and cut into fourths, lengthwise. Place the cucumbers, peas, scallions, salt and sugar in a saucepan. Cover with boiling water and simmer for 6 minutes. Drain the vegetables. Heat the butter in a skillet. Toss the vegetables in hot butter for 4 minutes until tender. Top with sour cream and season with freshly ground black pepper.
Hot cucumbers taste surprisingly good and are a pleasant change from cold sliced cucumbers.

Collard greens with cheese and eggs

6 servings

1¹/₂ pounds collard greens
¹/₂ cup water
¹/₂ teaspoon salt
4 strips bacon
1 tablespoon lemon juice
1 hard boiled egg,
 finely chopped
¹/₃ cup grated Parmesan cheese

Choose tender young, bright green collards. Strip the leaves from the veins. Wash carefully in plenty of cold water to remove the sand. Place in a large saucepan. Add the water and salt. Cover and steam the greens for 10 minutes until wilted and tender. Fry the bacon until all the fat has rendered. Drain and crumble the bacon. Transfer the greens to a serving dish. Add 2 tablespoons bacon fat and the lemon juice. Toss the greens. Garnish with crumbled bacon, chopped egg and Parmesan cheese.

In some southern homes the collard greens are cooked with a piece of fat back (pork) for many, many hours until they acquire a certain distinction, which can generally only be appreciated by fifth or sixth generation southerners.

Red cabbage with apple sauce

6 servings

1 small red cabbage
1 onion, finely chopped
1 cup chicken broth
¹/₂ cup applesauce
1 tablespoon red currant jelly
¹/₂ teaspoon salt
 Freshly ground black
 pepper
1 tablespoon cornstarch
 dissolved in
 2 tablespoons cold water

Remove the outer leaves and heavy stem of the cabbage. Shred into small pieces. Place the cabbage in a heavy casserole. Add the onion and chicken broth. Cover and simmer over low heat for 30 minutes. Stir in the applesauce, red currant jelly, salt and pepper and simmer another 20 minutes. Stir in cornstarch paste to form a sauce around the cabbage. Serve with roast pork.

Spring garden vegetables

6 servings

6 medium sized carrots
1 yellow onion
1 turnip
6 stalks celery
2 tablespoons butter
¹/₃ cup white vermouth
¹/₂ teaspoon salt
2 tablespoons finely chopped
 parsley

Peel the vegetables and cut each into slices and then into thin strips. Make all the strips as close to the same size as possible, about 4 inches long and ¹/₄ inch wide.

Melt the butter in a small casserole. Add the vermouth and all of the raw vegetables. Season with salt. Cover with a tight fitting lid. Simmer over very low heat for 25 minutes until all of the vegetables are tender. Garnish with parsley and serve with roast lamb.

As you will see there is very little liquid in this recipe, yet each vegetable emerges from the casserole, tender, fresh and bright in color. Each retains its own identity and flavor.

June peas

6 servings

    3 pounds peas in the pod
 ¹/₂ teaspoon salt
    1 teaspoon sugar
    2 sprigs fresh mint or
       ¹/₂ teaspoon dried
       mint
    1 tablespoon butter

Place the peas in a saucepan. Add enough boiling water to just cover them. Add the salt, sugar and mint. Boil gently, uncovered for 6 minutes until they are just tender. Drain and immediately rinse with cold water. Discard the fresh mint if used. Return the peas to the saucepan. Add the butter and cook over low heat until the peas are hot and shiny with butter.

The purpose of rinsing the peas or any other vegetable under cold water is to stop the cooking at the precise moment they are done. The splash of cold water brightens the color of the vegetable and crispens the texture. All vegetables can be cooked in advance in this way and need only to be plunged into boiling water or tossed with butted, at the last moment to reheat them.

Corn pudding

6 to 8 servings

    3 eggs
    2 tablespoons flour
 ³/₄ teaspoon salt
 ¹/₂ teaspoon paprika
 ¹/₂ teaspoon Worcestershire
       sauce
       Few drops Tabasco sauce
    1 cup heavy cream
    1 small onion, finely chopped
    3 tablespoons melted butter
    2 (12 ounce) cans corn
       Milk

Beat the eggs lightly in a mixing bowl. Add the flour, salt, paprika, Worcestershire sauce, Tabasco sauce, cream, onion and butter and beat until thoroughly combined. Drain the liquid from the cans of corn into a measuring cup. Add milk to make up 1 cup liquid. Beat the corn and liquid into the egg mixture. Pour into a 1¹/₂ quart mold. Place the mold in a larger pan of hot water to come halfway up the sides of the mold. Bake the pudding in a 350° oven 1¹/₄ hours. Remove from the oven and let stand 15 minutes before serving.

Corn fritters

6 servings

    2 cups corn niblets
    1 onion, finely chopped
    2 eggs, lightly beaten
 ¹/₄ cup milk
    1 cup flour
 ¹/₂ teaspoon paprika
    1 teaspoon baking powder
 ¹/₄ teaspoon salt
       Freshly ground black
       pepper
       Oil for deep frying

Combine corn, onion, eggs, milk, flour, paprika, baking powder, salt and pepper. Form the mixture into flat patties or small balls. Deep fry a few at a time about 3 minutes on each side. Drain on paper towels and serve with fried chicken.

Potatoes simmered in cream

6 servings

> 5 *large baking potatoes*
> 2 *cups heavy cream*
> 2 *tablespoons butter*
> 2 *cloves garlic, crushed*
> $^1/_2$ *teaspoon salt*
> $^1/_3$ *cup freshly grated Parmesan cheese Freshly ground black pepper*

Peel the potatoes and cut into very thin, uniform slices. Simmer the cream, butter, garlic and salt in a small saucepan until the quantity has reduced to $1^1/_2$ cups. Butter a small casserole and arrange the potatoes in layers. Between each layer add a little Parmesan cheese and freshly ground black pepper. Pour the reduced cream over the potatoes. Cover with a tight fitting lid and place in a preheated 350° oven for $1^1/_4$ hours until the potatoes are tender. Serve with roast meat. This is the most sublime of all potato dishes and if nobody else comes for dinner you can eat it all by yourself!

French fried potatoes

6 servings

> 6 *medium sized baking potatoes Oil or shortening for deep frying Coarse salt*

Peel the potatoes. Slice the potatoes lengthwise and cut into strips. Plunge the potatoes into a large bowl of iced water for 10 minutes. Drain and pat dry on paper towels.
Heat the fat to 375° on a deep frying thermometer. Lower a handful of potatoes carefully into the fat. Fry for about 8 minutes. Drain on paper towels. Continue until all the potatoes are partially cooked. Increase the heat to 400° and add the potatoes. Continue frying for 3 minutes until crisp and golden. Drain on paper towels. Sprinkle with coarse salt and serve immediately.
Note: Do not cover the potatoes with paper towels or they will steam and lose their crispness.

Sweet potato casserole

6 servings

> 4 *large sweet potatoes*
> 2 *tablespoons butter*
> 1 *(12 ounce) can crushed pineapple*
> 2 *tablespoons sherry or rum*
> $^1/_4$ *teaspoon nutmeg*
> $^1/_2$ *teaspoon cinnamon*
> 1 *teaspoon salt Freshly ground black pepper*

Boil the sweet potatoes in salted water for 30 minutes until tender. Drain and peel the potatoes. Mash the potatoes with the butter and stir in the drained crushed pineapple, sherry, nutmeg, cinnamon, salt and pepper. Fill into a buttered 6 cup casserole. Cover and bake in a preheated 350° oven for 15 minutes. It is traditional to top the sweet potatoes with an even layer of marshmallows.

Baked stuffed eggplant

6 servings

3 medium sized eggplants
4 teaspoons salt
5 tablespoons oil
1 onion, finely chopped
3 medium sized tomatoes, finely chopped
$^1/_4$ pound Swiss cheese, diced
Freshly ground black pepper

Cut the eggplants in half lengthwise. Scoop out the flesh and cut into small cubes. Reserve the shells. Place cubes on a wire rack and sprinkle with 3 teaspoons salt. Allow to stand undisturbed for 10 minutes to drain off the bitter juices. Rinse the eggplant and pat dry with paper towels. Heat 3 tablespoons of the oil in a large skillet. Add the onion and fry for 3 minutes. Add the eggplant and fry over moderately high heat for 6 minutes until lightly browned on all sides. Remove from the heat and stir in the tomatoes and cheese. Season with remaining salt and pepper. Divide the mixture between the eggplant shells. Place the shells in 2 baking dishes. Add 1 inch of boiling water to each dish. Sprinkle the filled shells with the remaining oil. Cover and bake in a preheated 350° oven for 30 minutes until the eggplant is soft and tender. Serve with roast meat or chicken.

Boston baked beans

10 servings

2 cups Great Northern beans
2 quarts cold water
1 onion, finely chopped
1 tablespoon tomato paste
1 tablespoon dry mustard
1 tablespoon Worcestershire sauce
1 teaspoon salt
$^1/_4$ teaspoon powdered cloves or
2 whole cloves
1 tablespoon vinegar
2 tablespoons dark molasses
6 slices bacon, cut into small pieces or
$^1/_4$ pound salt pork

Wash the beans and place them in a heavy casserole. Add water and bring to boiling point. Reduce the heat and simmer, uncovered, for 45 minutes. Remove the scum as it collects on the surface of the water. Add the remaining ingredients and stir into the beans gently. Cover and place in a preheated 300° oven for 2 hours. Remove the cover and continue cooking for 30 minutes until almost all the liquid has evaporated.

Artichokes vinaigrette

4 servings

Juice of $^1/_2$ lemon
1 teaspoon salt
4 globe artichokes

Vinaigrette sauce:
$^1/_2$ teaspoon salt
Freshly ground black pepper
1 clove garlic, crushed
$^1/_2$ teaspoon mild prepared mustard
2 tablespoons vinegar
6 tablespoons salad oil
3 tablespoons finely chopped parsley
3 tablespoons chopped chives
1 tablespoon capers
1 tablespoon chopped sweet gherkins
1 hard boiled egg, finely chopped

Bring a large pot of water to boiling point. Add the lemon juice and salt. Cut the stems from the artichokes and remove any discolored outer leaves. Plunge the artichokes into the water. Cover and simmer for 45 minutes or until a leaf can be pulled away from an artichoke easily. Drain the artichokes, squeezing out the excess water between 2 spatulas. In the meantime prepare the dressing by combining the dressing ingredients in the order listed. Divide the dressing between 6 small serving pots and serve the artichokes hot or cold. This is the closest you may come to paradise.

Baked acorn squash

4 servings

2 large acorn squash
2 tablespoons butter
1 cup applesauce
2 tablespoons maple syrup
1 teaspoon powdered ginger
1 bunch watercress

Cut each squash in half horizontally. Scoop out the membranes and seeds. Place the squash in a baking dish filled to a depth of 1 inch with boiling water. Place $^1/_4$ of the butter, applesauce, maple syrup and ginger in each cavity. Cover with aluminum foil and bake 35 minutes in a preheated 350° oven until tender. Drain off the water. Garnish with watercress and serve the squash from the baking dish.

Boston baked beans with steamed brown bread is a dish as American as Paul Revere. A bean pot simmering on the stove told colonial children that it was Sunday as surely as the calendar.

Acorn squash is a winter vegetable that stores well. Its fluted shape and rich color dress up the table and warm the heart on a crisp November evening.

The artichoke is among the most exciting of all vegetables to eat and serve. Since Cleopatra's day it has been used as a decorative motif in sculpture, architecture and furniture. Most of the artichokes in America are grown in the Salinas Valley along the coast of California, between San Francisco and Los Angeles.

Pickles

Originally, people like Peter Piper picked their peppers not only for pickling, but also to preserve them for the winter. Practically any food from, meats and fish to cauliflower, cucumber, nuts and melon rinds can be pickled. The ingredients are generally marinated in flavored vinegar or salt water and spices are added. The pickling time can vary from a few hours to several weeks. Chinese hundred-year-old eggs are at least six weeks old before they are eaten!
The American Puritans were particularly fond of pickles and served them frequently to remind everybody that into the sweetness of every life a little sourness will surely come. Apart from philosophical considerations, the pickles added flavor to a simple platter of sliced meats and provided interesting contrasts of taste and texture.
Many American recipes for pickles and relishes have been handed down from generation to generation and it has become traditional to welcome a new neighbor into the community with a gift of homemade pickles.

Artichoke pickle

Makes 3 pints

- 2 pounds Jerusalem artichokes
- 2 teaspoons lemon juice
- 2 cups water
- 2 onions, sliced
- 1 clove garlic, sliced
- 1½ cups sugar
- 1 teaspoon celery seed
- 1 teaspoon turmeric
- 1 teaspoon dry mustard
- 1½ teaspoons salt

Wash and peel the artichokes. Cut into thin slices. Add lemon juice and water to prevent discoloring. Drain the artichokes and pack into sterilized jars with the onions and garlic. Combine the sugar, celery seed, turmeric, mustard and salt in a saucepan. Bring to a boil, reduce the heat and simmer for 2 or 3 minutes. Cool. Pour over the artichokes and seal the jars. Keep 2 months before serving.

Cranberry relish

Makes 6 cups

- 4 cups cranberries
- 2 oranges
- 2 cups sugar

Wash the cranberries and put through a food grinder. Grind the oranges or chop into small pieces, chopping through the rind. Remove the seeds and squeeze the juice over the cranberries. Combine chopped oranges with the cranberries. Add the sugar and mix well. Pour into covered jars and refrigerate for 48 hours before using. Serve with meat or poultry.

Corn relish

Makes 5 pints

- 12 ears of corn
- 1 head green cabbage, chopped
- 4 large onions, chopped
- 2 green peppers, seeded
- 2 red peppers, seeded
- 1 tablespoon celery seed
- 1 tablespoon dry mustard
- 1 tablespoon salt
- 1 cup sugar
- 1 tablespoon flour
- 1 teaspoon turmeric
- 6 cups vinegar

Cut the corn from the cobs. Chop the cabbage, onions and peppers finely and mix with the corn. Combine the celery seed, mustard, salt, sugar, flour, turmeric and vinegar and stir to form a smooth dressing. Add the chopped vegetables, bring to a boil, reduce the heat and simmer slowly for 20 to 30 minutes, stirring occasionally. Pack in hot sterilized jars and seal.

Mustard pickle

Makes 8 pints

- 4 cucumbers, sliced
- 2 cups small white onions, peeled and chopped
- 2 cups small green tomatoes, cut into eighths
- 2 cups cauliflower flowerets
- 2 red peppers, cut into $1/4$ inch slices
- 2 green peppers, cut into $1/4$ inch slices
- 1 cup sliced carrots
- 1 cup coarse salt
- 2 quarts cold water
- 3 cups vinegar
- $1^1/4$ cups sugar
- $1/2$ cup flour
- 2 teaspoons turmeric
- 1 teaspoon celery salt
- 4 tablespoons dry mustard

Place all the vegetables in a large bowl and cover with the salt dissolved in the water. Cover and chill for 24 hours, turning the vegetables in the brine occasionally. Drain the vegetables. Combine the vinegar, sugar, flour, turmeric, celery salt and mustard and mix to form a smooth paste. Bring to a boil, add the drained vegetables and cook, uncovered, for 10 minutes, stirring constantly. Pour into sterilized jars and seal. Process in a boiling water bath for 10 minutes (see recipe page 60 for Cauliflower pickle). Serve with cold meats after 24 hours.

Pickled beets

Makes 2 pints

- 4 cups cooked, sliced beets
- 1 onion, peeled and thinly sliced
- 2 cups vinegar
- 4 tablespoons sugar
- $1/2$ teaspoon salt
- 2 tablespoons prepared horseradish
- 1 teaspoon cinnamon
- $1/2$ teaspoon nutmeg
- 1 teaspoon mustard seed
- 6 whole cloves
- 1 teaspoon celery seed

Place the beets and onion in clean hot jars. Combine the vinegar, sugar, salt and horseradish. Add the spices and bring to a boil. Pour over the beets and seal the jars. Let stand for 2 days before using.

Dill pickles

Makes 4 pints

- 3 pounds small cucumbers
- 8 sprigs fresh dill weed
- 4 cloves garlic
- 4 cups water
- 2 tablespoons vinegar
- $1/2$ cup coarse salt
- 1 teaspoon whole pickling spice
- $1/2$ teaspoon mustard seed
- 6 peppercorns

Wash the cucumbers and dill. Cut the cucumbers into quarters lengthwise and pack into sterilized jars with dill and the garlic.
Combine the water, vinegar and salt and bring to a boil. Add the pickling spice, mustard seed and peppercorns. Pour over the cucumbers, making sure they are well covered. Seal and allow to stand for a week. Use within 2 to 3 weeks.

Sweet cucumber pickles

Makes 6 pints

- 6 pounds small cucumbers, washed and sliced
- 4 onions, sliced or chopped
- $1/2$ cup salt
- 4 cups vinegar
- 3 cups sugar
- 1 teaspoon whole cloves
- 1 tablespoon mustard seed
- 1 teaspoon peppercorns

Sprinkle the cucumbers and onion with the salt and allow to stand for 24 hours. Drain well and place in a large pan. Add the vinegar, sugar, cloves, mustard seed and peppercorns. Bring to a boil and simmer for 3 minutes. Pack into hot sterilized jars, filling to the brim with the syrup. Seal. Process in a hot water bath for 10 minutes (See recipe for Cauliflower pickle on page 60.)

Almost everybody has a favorite pickle or relish recipe handed down through the family. Here are some old-time reliables: (clockwise from top): Artichoke Pickles, Corn relish, Cranberry relish (recipe page 58), Mustard pickle, Pickled beets, Dill pickles and Sweet cucumber pickle (recipes page 59).

Cauliflower pickle

Cauliflower pickle

Makes 6 pints

    2 large cauliflowers
        (about 4 pounds)
    1 cup coarse salt
    8 cups water
    4 cups vinegar
$^1/_2$ cup sugar
    1 teaspoon salt
    3 tablespoons horseradish
    2 teaspoons cinnamon
    1 tablespoon black
        peppercorns
    1 tablespoon mustard seed
   12 whole cloves
    1 teaspoon celery seed

Break the heads into small flowerets. Place in a large bowl. Dissolve the salt in the water, pour over the cauliflower and leave for 24 hours. Drain thoroughly and rinse well. Pack into sterilized jars. Mix the vinegar, sugar, salt and horseradish. Heat to boiling. Tie the spices in a cheesecloth bag and allow to steep in the hot vinegar for 2 hours. Remove the spices, pour the vinegar over the cauliflower to cover. Seal the jars. Process in a hot water bath for 15 minutes. To process in a hot water bath: Place the jars on a rack in a deep kettle of boiling water so they are covered by 1 inch of water (the jars should not touch each other). Cover the kettle with a tight fitting lid and bring water to a boil. Boil gently for the specific time in each recipe. Remove the jars immediately, tighten the seal and cool.

Preserves

Dust off grandmother's mason jars and lay down a store of whatever is in season for gifts, garnishes and good pure taste. Here, for example, are:

Cherry preserves (recipe page 62), Strawberry preserves, Fruit Marmalades and Apple butter (recipe page 63).

The word marmalade comes from the Portuguese word 'marmelado' which is a preserve made from quinces or 'marmelos.' In France 'marmelade' is a purée of stewed fruit and in Spain the same word is given to a confection made by combining fruit and cheese. In 1797 a Scotsman named John Keiller developed a recipe for orange marmalade which spread his name and preserves far beyond his native land.

Homemade marmalades, jellies and fruit butters capture the summer sun in a jar. They are surprisingly easy to make and last for a long time, so they are well worth the effort. Strawberry preserves have always been popular in America.

In Europe in the 1500's, strawberries were so rare and costly that they were counted one by one and sold threaded onto a long piece of straw. Maybe this is how they got their name, though it may also be because a bed of straw was, and is still used to protect the berries from being splashed with mud during summer showers. Wild beach plum jelly is a Massachusetts specialty, while the Pennsylvania Dutch have a particular affection for apple butter. Their first food in America, after a long and difficult journey, consisted of fresh apples and clear spring water. Each year, since their arrival in 1734, a Thanksgiving celebration is recreated with a meal of bread, apple butter and water.

Wild beach plum jelly

2 quarts ripe beach plums
*1 quart underripe beach
plums*
*1 tart green apple, cut into
wedges
Water
Sugar*

Place the plums, apple and water
to barely cover the fruit in a large
saucepan. Bring to a boil and
cook 15 minutes until the plums
are softened. Bruise them with a
wooden spatula and continue
cooking 10 to 15 minutes until
very soft. Strain the juice
through several layers of
cheesecloth. When the juice has
dripped through, gather the pulp
up in the cheesecloth and squeeze
it very lightly. The jelly will be
cloudy if the pulp is squeezed too
much. Measure the juice and
pour it into a saucepan. Add 2/3
cup sugar for each cup of juice.
Stir the mixture over medium
heat until the sugar dissolves.
Boil rapidly until setting point is
reached. To test for setting, see
Plum preserves recipe on this
page. Cool the jelly slightly.
Pour into hot sterilized jelly
glasses and seal.

Cherry preserves

Makes 4 pints

*4 pounds tart cherries,
weighed after stoning*
6 cups sugar

Place the stoned cherries and
sugar in a large pan. Cook over a
low heat, stirring frequently until
the sugar has dissolved and the
juice runs freely from the fruit.
Bring to a boil and boil rapidly
until setting point is reached.
Pour into dry sterilized glasses
and seal with melted wax.
Test for setting as for Plum
preserves (recipe this page).

Plum preserves

Makes 6 pints

6 pounds plums
2¹/₂ cups water
10 cups sugar
¹/₃ cup lemon juice

Wash the plums and place in a
large saucepan with the water.
Bring to a boil, reduce the heat
and simmer until the plums are
soft. Add the sugar and lemon
juice. Bring to a boil again and
boil rapidly until setting point is
reached. Pour into dry, sterilized
glasses and seal with melted wax.
To test for setting, place a little
jam on a saucer and leave in the
refrigerator for 5 minutes. If a
skin has formed that wrinkles
when moved the jam is ready. Do
not boil rapidly while this test is
being made, as the jam will
continue to set.

Strawberry preserves

Makes 4 pints

    4 *cups fresh strawberries*
    5 *cups sugar*
    3 *tablespoons lemon juice*

Rinse the strawberries briefly and remove the stems. Place alternate layers of sugar and berries in a large saucepan. Cook over a very low heat until the sugar has dissolved and bring to a boil slowly. Boil briskly for 9 minutes. Remove from the heat, add the lemon juice and leave to stand overnight to allow the berries to absorb the syrup. The next day, bring to a boil and boil for 9 minutes. Leave to cool. Pour into dry, sterilized glasses and seal with melted wax.
Note: Use local strawberries that are fully ripened on the vine as only mature fruit contains enough pectin to set the preserves.

Grapefruit marmalade

Makes 6 pints

    4 *grapefruit*
    1 *tablespoon citric acid*
    8 *cups water*
    12 *cups sugar*

Wash the grapefruit. Pare the colored rind and cut it into thin strips. Discard the white pith beneath the rind. Cut each grapefruit in half. Squeeze and reserve the juice and seeds. Tie the seeds in a piece of cheesecloth. Place the strips of rind, seeds in their cheesecloth bag, grapefruit juice, citric acid and 8 cups water in a large saucepan. Let stand overnight. Bring the mixture to a boil, lower the heat and simmer 1 hour. Remove the bag of seeds. Stir in the sugar until dissolved. Boil rapidly until setting point is reached. To test for setting, see Plum preserve (recipe page 62). Cool the marmalade slightly. Pour into sterilized jelly glasses and seal.

Orange marmalade

Makes 6 pints

    3 *large Valencia oranges*
    4 *small lemons*
    16 *cups water*
    12 *cups sugar*

Wash the oranges and lemons and cut them in half. Remove and reserve the seeds from the fruit. Squeeze the juice into a large saucepan. Tie the seeds in a cheesecloth bag and add the seeds and water to the fruit juice. Discard the white pith from the orange and lemon rind and add the rind to the saucepan. Let the mixture stand 24 hours. Bring to a boil, lower the heat and simmer 1 hour. Remove the rind and cut it into very thin shreds. Return the shredded rind to the saucepan. Discard the bag of seeds. Add the sugar to the fruit mixture and stir over medium heat until dissolved. Boil rapidly until setting point is reached. To test for setting, see Plum preserves, recipe on page 62. Cool the marmalade 10 minutes. Pour into sterilized jelly glasses and seal.

Apple butter

Makes 10 cups

    6 *pounds tart apples*
    8 *cups sweet cider*
    1 *cinnamon stick*
    6 *cloves*
       Rind of 1 lemon
    3 *cups sugar*

Wash the apples and cut into quarters. Combine the apples and cider in a large pan and cook until the apples are tender. Force through a sieve. Boil the pulp until thick enough to heap on a spoon, stirring frequently to prevent sticking. Tie the cinnamon stick, cloves and lemon rind in a square of cheesecloth and add to the pulp with the sugar. Continue cooking slowly about 1 hour, stirring frequently. Remove the cheesecloth bag of spices. Place about $1/4$ cup of the apple purée on a plate, and allow it to stand undisturbed for 3 minutes. If there are no free flowing juices the apple butter is ready. Pour into hot sterilized jars immediately and seal.

Desserts

The key to this pie's name is that the limes it was originally made with, grew on a chain of wind-washed, sun-drenched coral islands stretching from the tip of Florida into the Caribbean Sea, called the 'cays' but pronounced 'keys.' These limes are incredibly juicy miracles of flavor.

Key lime pie

Key lime pie

8 servings

1	*(9 inch) deep baked pie shell*
4	*eggs, separated*
$^1/_2$	*cup sugar*
	Grated rind of 3 limes
$^1/_3$	*cup lime juice*
1	*cup heavy cream*
$1^1/_2$	*packages gelatin*
$^1/_3$	*cup water*

Beat the egg yolks and sugar together until they are very thick and lemon colored. Add the grated rind of 2 limes. Add the lime juice gradually and continue beating until the mixture is thick. Beat the cream until it is the same consistency as the yolk mixture. Sprinkle the gelatin over the cold water in a small saucepan. Allow the gelatin to stand undisturbed for 5 minutes. Place over low heat until hot but not boiling. Remove the dissolved gelatin from the heat. Beat the egg whites until they stand in soft peaks. Fold the gelatin into the lime cream mixture and then fold in the beaten egg-whites immediately. (The mixture will begin to set almost at once.) Pour the mixture into the pie shell. Smooth the surface with a knife and chill in the refrigerator at least 4 hours before serving. Decorate with the remaining grated lime rind.
The lime mixture can also be served as a cold souffle. It freezes well.

A cheese cake is one of the few dishes that can make or break a restaurant, delicatessen or hostess. You can count on this recipe to be a success.

The lightest meringue, shaded with the most delicate tinge of brown, the least cornstarch, the truest lemon flavor and the flakiest crust win the pie-baking contests (recipe page 83).

Cheese cake

Crust:
- 1 tablespoon butter
- 2 cups graham cracker crumbs
- $1/4$ cup sugar
- 4 tablespoons butter, melted
- $1/2$ teaspoon cinnamon

Cheese filling:
- 3 (8 ounce) packages Philadelphia cream cheese
- 1 cup sugar
- 2 whole eggs
- 2 egg yolks
- Grated rind and juice of 2 lemons
- 1 tablespoon vanilla
- $1/2$ cup sour cream

To prepare the crust, butter a 4 inch deep and 8 inch wide cake tin generously. In a bowl, combine the graham cracker crumbs, sugar, butter and cinnamon. Press the crumbs into the bottom and sides of the cake tin.

To prepare the filling, beat the cheese in a mixer until softened. Beat in the sugar. Beat in the eggs and egg yolks, 1 at a time. Add the grated lemon rind, lemon juice and vanilla. Fold in the sour cream.

Fill the graham cracker crust with the filling. Bake in a preheated 350° oven for 1 hour. Chill at least 4 hours before serving.

Sunshine cake with fresh lemon icing

3 eggs, separated
³/₄ cup cold water
1¹/₄ cups sugar
1¹/₂ cups sifted cake
   flour
1 teaspoon vanilla
¹/₄ teaspoon salt
¹/₄ teaspoon cream of
   tartar

Icing:
1¹/₂ cups sugar
¹/₂ teaspoon salt
¹/₄ teaspoon cream of
   tartar
   Grated rind of
   1 large lemon
3 tablespoons fresh
   lemon juice
2 egg whites
2 tablespoons water

Place the egg yolks and water in the bowl of an electric mixer and beat until the mixture has increased to about 4 cups. Add the sugar gradually beating constantly. When all the sugar has been added, continue to beat about 7 minutes longer. Set the mixer at the lowest speed and fold in the flour and vanilla just until the flour is incorporated. Beat the egg whites with the salt and cream of tartar until stiff peaks form. Carefully fold the egg whites into the batter. Spoon the batter into an ungreased angel cake pan and bake in a preheated 325° about 1 hour. Invert the pan and let the cake hang until cold. To prepare the icing, place all the ingredients in a heavy saucepan or in the top of a double boiler and beat constantly over low heat with an electric hand mixer or rotary beater until the mixture stands in peaks. Remove the cake from the pan and place on a serving plate. Spread the top and sides of the cake with fresh lemon icing.

Peach cobbler

6 servings

4 cups sliced peaches
1 tablespoon cornstarch
¹/₂ cup sugar
1 cup water
¹/₂ teaspoon almond essence
2 tablespoons butter
1 cup flour
1 teaspoon baking powder
¹/₂ teaspoon salt
1 tablespoons sugar
2 tablespoons butter
3 tablespoons milk

Place the sliced peaches in a saucepan. Mix the cornstarch and sugar with the water and pour over the peaches. Bring to a boil and simmer until the sauce thickens. Add the almond essence. Pour the hot fruit and sauce into a buttered 6 cup casserole and dot with the butter. Sift the flour, baking powder and salt and add the sugar. Cut in the butter with a pastry blender and stir in the milk. Turn the dough onto a floured board, knead lightly and pat into shape to fit over the peaches. Bake in a preheated 425° oven for 30 minutes. Serve warm with vanilla ice cream.

Pecan pie

8 servings

5 eggs
¹/₄ cup sugar
1 teaspoon vanilla extract
2 tablespoons butter, melted
¹/₂ cup sifted flour
2 cups dark corn syrup
¹/₂ recipe for pastry for
   apple pie on page 68
1 cup pecan halves
1 cup whipped cream

Beat together the eggs and sugar in a bowl. Stir in the vanilla extract, butter, flour and corn syrup. Fill into an unbaked 9″ pastry shell. Top with pecan halves. Place the pie plate on a cookie sheet in a preheated 350° oven for 40 minutes until the filling has set. Chill in the refrigerator at least 4 hours before serving. Decorate the pie with rosettes of whipped cream or serve the cream separately.

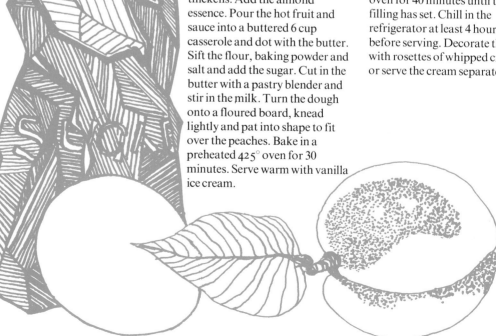

Apple brown Betty

6 servings

    5 *tablespoons butter*
1¼ *cups graham cracker
        crumbs*
    4 *medium sized cooking
        apples*
        *Grated rind and juice of
        1 lemon*
 ½ *cup brown sugar*
    1 *teaspoon cinnamon*
 ½ *teaspoon powdered cloves*
 ¼ *teaspoon nutmeg*
 ⅓ *cup water or apple cider*
    1 *teaspoon vanilla*

Melt the butter in a small
saucepan. Combine the cracker
crumbs with the butter. Butter a
1 quart baking dish and place a
layer of ⅓ of the cracker
crumbs on the bottom. Peel, core
and slice the apples thinly and
place in a bowl. Add the
remaining ingredients. Toss the
mixture lightly to combine. Place
half of the apple mixture over the
layer of cracker crumbs. Repeat
these 2 layers. Add liquid
remaining in the bowl and top
with the remaining ⅓ of the
cracker crumbs. Cover with foil
and bake in a preheated 350°
oven for 45 minutes. Discard the
foil and continue baking for 10
minutes until the crumbs are
crisp and lightly browned.
This dessert can be made with
any other fruits in season, such as
peaches, blueberries or cherries.

Chocolate cake

Makes 2 8-inch layers

 ½ *cup butter*
1¼ *cups sugar*
    2 *eggs, beaten*
    2 *envelopes redi-blend
        unsweetened chocolate*
1¾ *cups sifted cake flour*
 ½ *teaspoon salt*
1½ *teaspoons baking powder*
    1 *cup milk*
    1 *teaspoon vanilla*

Almond filling:
 ½ *cup sugar*
    3 *tablespoons flour*
 ¼ *teaspoon salt*
1½ *cups milk*
    2 *egg yolks, beaten*
    1 *teaspoon almond essence*

Frosting:
    4 *tablespoons butter*
1½ *cups sifted powdered
        sugar*
    1 *teaspoon vanilla essence*
    3 *envelopes redi-blend
        unsweetened chocolate*
 ¼ *teaspoon salt*
    2 *egg whites, stiffly beaten*

Beat the butter and sugar until
light and fluffy. Add the beaten
eggs gradually and mix in the
chocolate. Sift the flour, salt and
baking powder together and add
to the butter mixture alternately
with the milk. Add the vanilla.
Pour into 2 buttered and floured
8 inch round cake pans. Bake in a
preheated 350° oven for 35
minutes. Turn out onto a cake
rack to cool.
Filling: Combine the sugar, flour

and salt in the top of a double
boiler. Add the milk and mix
thoroughly. Place over boiling
water and cook for 10 minutes,
stirring constantly. Pour a small
amount of the mixture over the
egg yolks, stir well and return to
the double boiler. Cook 2
minutes. Add the almond
essence and allow to cool. When
cool, spread between the
chocolate cake layers.
Frosting: Beat the butter with ¾
cup of the powdered sugar until
light and fluffy. Add the vanilla,
chocolate and salt. Add the
remaining sugar to the beaten
egg whites 2 tablespoons at a
time and beat until the mixture
will stand in peaks. Add to the
chocolate mixture, folding in
gently but thoroughly only
enough to blend. Cover the top
and sides of the filled chocolate
cake and refrigerate for 30
minutes.

Pound cake
with chocolate sauce

Makes 2 pound cakes

    2 *cups butter*
    2 *cups sugar*
    8 *large eggs*
    5 *cups sifted cake flour*
 ½ *teaspoon salt*
    1 *teaspoon lemon extract*
        Grated rind of 1 lemon

Sauce:
    1 *cup milk*
    4 *squares unsweetened
        chocolate*
 ¼ *teaspoon salt*
    2 *cups sugar*
 ¼ *cup light corn syrup*
1½ *tablespoons butter*
 ½ *teaspoon vanilla*

Beat the butter until light and
fluffy and add the sugar
gradually. Add the eggs, 1 at a
time, beating well after each
addition. Sift the flour and salt
together and add to the butter
mixture a few spoonfuls at a
time, mixing just enough to
blend. Add the lemon extract
and rind. Transfer to 2 buttered
and floured 9 × 5 × 3 inch loaf
pans. Bake in a preheated 275°
oven for 2½ hours. Cool 10
minutes, remove from the pans
and cool on cake racks.
Sauce: Combine the milk and
chocolate in a pan and heat until
the chocolate melts. Beat until
smooth and add the salt, sugar
and corn syrup. Bring to a boil,
stirring constantly, and cook for
5 minutes. Remove from the
heat, stir in the butter and vanilla
and serve hot. Makes 2 cups.

Pound cake was made originally with a pound of butter, a pound of flour, a pound of eggs and a pound of sugar. This is a lighter, modern version: (recipe page 67, 4th column). If you prefer to serve it plain, save the chocolate sauce for a bowl of ice cream.

Apple pie, mom and taxes are at the heart of American life. The best pies were invented before income taxes and still come from the tartest apples and the sweetest moms.

Apple pie

Pastry:
- 2¹/₂ *cups all purpose flour*
- ¹/₄ *teaspoon salt*
- 6 *tablespoons butter*
- 6 *tablespoons margarine or solid shortening*
- 8 *to 10 tablespoons cold water*

Filling:
- 6 *medium sized baking apples*
- 1 *tablespoon cornstarch dissolved in*
- 2 *tablespoons cold water*
- 2 *tablespoons sugar*
- ¹/₄ *teaspoon nutmeg*
- ¹/₂ *teaspoon cinnamon*
- 1 *tablespoon butter*

Glaze:
- 1 *egg yolk*
- 2 *tablespoons heavy cream or milk*
- *Powdered sugar*

To prepare the pastry, sift the flour and measure into a bowl. Add the salt. Cut the butter into small pieces and combine the butter and flour with the fingertips or a pastry blender. When the pieces of butter are about the size of small peas, add the margarine and blend with a pastry blender. Stir in 8 tablespoons water with a fork. Add remaining water if necessary to form the dough into a ball. Wrap the pastry in waxed paper and chill for 20 minutes. Cut the dough in half and roll on a floured board. Fit the first half of the pastry into a deep 9 or 10 inch pie plate.

To prepare the filling, peel, core and slice the apples thinly. Fill the pie plate with apples. Add remaining filling ingredients and cover with remaining pastry. Cut several small slashes in the pastry cover to allow steam to escape. To prepare the glaze, combine the egg yolk and cream and brush the pastry with the mixture.

Bake the pie in a preheated 375° oven for 35 minutes until pastry is golden. Dust with sifted powdered sugar. Serve with sweetened whipped cream, ice cream or slices of sharp cheddar cheese.

Aztec Indians thought chocolate was too stimulating for unmarried women. Its rich flavor has made chocolate America's favorite ice cream (recipe page 70).

Chocolate ice cream

Makes 1 1/2 quarts

3/4 cup sugar
1/3 cup water
1/4 teaspoon cream of tartar
4 egg yolks
6 ounces semi-sweet chocolate pieces
3 tablespoons water
3 cups heavy cream

Place the sugar, water and cream of tartar in a saucepan. Boil until the syrup registers 230° on a candy thermometer. In the meantime, beat the egg yolks until very thick. Add the boiling syrup to the egg yolks in a thin stream of droplets while beating constantly. Do not add the syrup too quickly or the egg yolks will scramble. Continue beating until the mixture has doubled in bulk. Melt the chocolate in 3 tablespoons water in a small saucepan. Stir the chocolate into the egg mixture with a spoon. Stir in the cream. Fill an ice cream freezer. Pack crushed ice alternately with 3 layers of 1 grain thick rock salt. Churn the ice cream and freeze until firm. There are other recipes for chocolate ice cream which contain less cream, but they are not as good.

Gingerbread

2 eggs
1/4 cup dark brown sugar
3/4 cup dark molasses
1/2 cup butter
1 cup boiling water
2 1/2 cups flour
1/2 teaspoon baking powder
2 teaspoons baking soda
2 teaspoons powdered ginger
1 1/2 teaspoons cinnamon
1/2 teaspoon nutmeg
1/2 teaspoon powdered cloves

Beat together the eggs and sugar until very thick. Stir in the molasses. Cut the butter into small pieces and melt in boiling water. Sift together the flour, baking powder, baking soda, ginger, cinnamon, nutmeg and cloves. Add the dry ingredients alternately with the water to the egg mixture. Beat the batter well after each addition. Pour the batter into a buttered and floured 8 × 8 × 2 inch baking pan. Bake in a preheated 400° oven for 35 minutes or until a cake tester inserted into the center comes out clean. Let the gingerbread cool for 15 minutes and cut into squares.

Coconut cake

24 2-inch squares

1/2 cup butter
1 1/2 cups sugar
2 cups sifted cake flour
2 teaspoons baking powder
1/2 teaspoon salt
3/4 cup milk
1 teaspoon vanilla
3/4 cup sweetened flaked coconut
4 egg whites, siffly beaten

Frosting:
1/3 cup butter
3/4 cup brown sugar
3/4 cup sweetened flaked coconut
1/2 cup chopped walnuts
2 tablespoons heavy cream

Beat the butter and sugar until very light and creamy. Sift the flour, baking powder and salt and add to the butter mixture alternately with the milk. Add the vanilla and coconut. Gently fold in the beaten egg whites. Pour into a buttered 8 × 12 × 2 inch baking pan. Bake in a preheated 350° oven for 30 minutes. Cool for 15 minutes. **Frosting:** Combine all the ingredients in a saucepan and heat until the butter and sugar are melted. Spread on the cooled cake and place in a 400° oven for 6 minutes until lightly browned. Cut into squares when cool.

Strawberry shortcake

6 servings

2 cups sifted all purpose flour
4 teaspoons baking powder
1/2 teaspoon salt
6 tablespoons sugar
4 tablespoons butter
4 tablespoons shortening
2/3 cup milk

2 pints ripe strawberries
1 tablespoon sugar
1 1/2 cups heavy cream

Sift the flour, baking powder, salt and sugar together into a bowl. Cut the butter and shortening into the flour mixture with a pastry blender or 2 knives until the mixture resembles coarse meal. Add the milk and stir the dough with a fork into a ball. Turn the dough out on a floured board and knead. Roll or pat the dough to a 1 inch thickness. Cut into 6 rounds. Place the rounds in an ungreased baking pan and bake in a 450° oven 15 minutes. Remove from the oven and let cool. Slice the strawberries. Sprinkle the strawberries with 1 tablespoon sugar. Beat the cream until it thickens slightly but is still of pouring consistency. Using a fork, split each shortcake in half and place the bottom halves on individual serving plates. Spoon the sliced strawberries over the cakes and top with the remaining cake halves. Decorate with whole strawberries and pour a little cream over the shortcakes.

Indian pudding

6 servings

> 4 cups milk
> $^1/_4$ cup cornmeal
> 2 eggs
> 2 tablespoons molasses
> $^1/_2$ cup dark brown sugar,
>   firmly packed
> $^1/_2$ teaspoon salt
> $^1/_2$ teaspoon ground ginger
> $^1/_2$ teaspoon cinnamon
> 4 tablespoons butter, cut
>   into small pieces
> $^3/_4$ cup raisins

Heat $3^1/_2$ cups milk in a heavy saucepan. Combine the remaining milk with the cornmeal and add to the hot milk. Stir constantly until the mixture begins to simmer. Cook over the lowest possible heat 20 minutes, stirring occasionally. Meanwhile beat the eggs lightly in a small bowl and stir in the molasses, brown sugar, salt, ginger and cinnamon. Remove the milk mixture from the heat and stir in the butter and raisins. Add the egg mixture and combine thoroughly. Pour into a $1^1/_2$ quart baking dish and bake in a 325° oven 1 to $1^1/_4$ hours until the pudding is set. Serve warm with a pitcher of fresh cream.

Brownies

Makes 16 2-inch squares

> 2 squares unsweetened
>   baking chocolate
> $^1/_3$ cup butter
> 1 cup sugar
> 2 eggs, beaten
> $^3/_4$ cup flour
> $^1/_2$ teaspoon salt
> $^1/_2$ teaspoon baking powder
> $^1/_2$ cup chopped walnuts

Melt the chocolate and butter in the top of a double boiler. Remove from the heat. Beat in the sugar and eggs and stir until smooth. Sift together the flour, salt and baking powder and fold into the chocolate mixture. Add the chopped walnuts. Turn into a buttered 8-inch square baking pan and bake in a preheated 350° oven for 30 minutes. Cut into squares when cool.

Chocolate chip cookies

Makes 4 dozen $2^1/_2$ inch cookies

> $^1/_2$ cup butter
> $^1/_4$ cup white sugar
> $^1/_2$ cup brown sugar
> 1 egg
> $1^1/_4$ cups flour
> $^1/_2$ teaspoon salt
> $^1/_2$ teaspoon baking soda
>   Grated rind of 1 orange
> $^3/_4$ cup chocolate chips
> $^1/_2$ cup chopped walnuts

Beat the butter, white and brown sugar until light and creamy. Add the egg and beat until fluffy. Sift the flour, salt and baking soda together and add to the creamed mixture. Add the grated orange rind and stir in the chocolate chips and walnuts. Drop teaspoonfuls of the mixture onto a buttered cookie sheet and bake in a preheated 375° oven for 10 to 12 minutes until golden brown. Remove from the cookie sheet while warm and cool on a wire rack.

Chocolate fudge cookies

4 dozen cookies

> $^1/_2$ cup butter
> $1^1/_4$ cups brown sugar,
>   firmly packed
> 2 eggs
> 4 tablespoons unsweetened
>   cocoa
> $1^1/_2$ cups sifted all purpose
>   flour
> 1 teaspoon vanilla
> 1 cup chopped pecans or
>   walnuts

Beat the butter until creamy. Add the sugar gradually and continue beating until the mixture is light and fluffy. Add the eggs, 1 at a time, beating well after each addition. Beat in the cocoa and flour gradually. Add the vanilla and combine thoroughly. Fold in the chopped nuts. Drop the batter from a teaspoon onto buttered cookie sheets. Bake in a 350° oven 12 minutes. Cool on wire racks.

Chocolate chip cookies may have overtaken apple pie as the most popular American homemade, year-round dessert (recipe page 71, 3rd column).

Brownies: simple, rich and nutty, that can be made by children, will disappear fast and raise lots of money for the Girl Scouts (recipe page 71, 2nd column).

When children are ready to graduate from making fudge by themselves, show them the recipe on page 71 for Fudge Cookies, and it will open up a whole new world.

Honey-glazed doughnuts, crispy and sweet, are still warm when the children come home from school.

Waffles

Honey dipped doughnuts

6 servings

4 eggs, separated
1 teaspoon sugar
2 cups milk
$^1/_2$ cup melted butter
2 cups sifted all
   purpose flour
4 teaspoons baking powder
$^1/_4$ teaspoon salt

Beat the egg yolks with the sugar until thick. Stir in the milk and butter. Sift together the flour, baking powder and salt. Gradually add the flour to the milk mixture, beating until smooth. Beat the egg whites until stiff. Stir $^1/_3$ of the whites into the batter and carefully fold in the remainder. Ladle about 1 cup of the batter onto a hot waffle iron and bake about 7 minutes. If the waffle is not done, it will tend to stick to the iron when the lid is lifted.
Serve immediately with melted butter and warm maple syrup at breakfast. For dessert, top with ice cream.

Makes 3 dozen

1 cup lukewarm milk
2 packages dry yeast
3 tablespoons sugar
1 teaspoon salt
2 eggs, lightly beaten
1 teaspoon cinnamon
4 cups flour
   Oil for deep frying
1 cup honey
$^1/_2$ cup boiling water

Pour the milk into a large bowl. Stir in the yeast, sugar and salt and let the mixture stand for 5 minutes. Stir in the eggs and cinnamon. Add 3 cups flour and stir to form a medium thick dough. Add the remaining flour a little at a time, kneading the dough until it is smooth and elastic and no longer sticky. Place the dough in an oiled bowl. Cover and leave in a warm place until doubled in bulk. Punch the dough down and knead it lovingly for a couple of minutes. Cover and leave the dough to rise again until doubled in bulk. Knead the dough and roll it on a floured board. Cut the dough with a floured doughnut cutter, or pinch off small pieces of dough and form into balls. Leave the dough to rest for 30 minutes.

Deep fry the doughnuts in hot oil for 5 minutes until puffed and golden. Dip the dough in honey combined with enough hot water to form a thick syrup. Drain the doughnuts on a wire rack.

Fruits

Specific fruits conjure up all sorts of images. If it was an apple that caused Adam's downfall; it seems odd to conclude that an apple a day keeps the doctor away. Figs seem to be inescapably linked with the decadence of the falling Roman empire, while peaches and cream evoke visions of fresh young maidens dancing in the morning dew by dawn's early light. Strawberries herald the summer sunshine, but tangerines, though they are now available in the middle of the year, are an integral part of Christmas and flickering winter firelight.
Of course any fresh fruits can be put together to make a fruit salad and they will taste as delicious as a collection of flowers picked at random from a country garden. But those that are all in season together form the most exquisite of harmonious flavors. Winter citrus fruits and apples make as natural a grouping as a bowl of berries in June.

Plum compote

6 servings

> 2 pounds plums
> 1/4 cup water
> 1/4 cup sugar
> Grated rind and juice of 1 orange
> 1/2 cup port wine
> 2 tablespoons red currant jelly
> 1/2 teaspoon almond extract
> 1/2 cup sliced almonds

Remove the pits from the plums and place the plums in a saucepan. Add all the remaining ingredients except the almond extract and almonds. Cover and simmer over low heat for 15 minutes until the fruit is soft but still holding its shape. Add the almond extract. Chill 4 hours before serving. Scatter almonds over the fruit.

Baked apples with honey

4 servings

> 4 baking apples
> 4 teaspoons butter
> 4 teaspoons seedless raisins
> 4 teaspoons honey
> 4 teaspoons brown sugar
> 1 cup apple cider

Peel the top half of each apple and remove the cores. Arrange the apples in a baking dish and place a teaspoon of butter, raisins, honey and brown sugar in each cavity. Pour cider into the dish. Bake the apples for 25 to 30 minutes, until tender, basting with the cider occasionally. Serve with ice cream.
The apples are equally good served hot or cold.

Baked peaches

4 servings

> 4 beautiful ripe peaches
> 2 cups water
> 1 cup sugar
> 4 tablespoons finely chopped almonds
> 2 sugar cookies, crumbled
> 4 tablespoons sherry or rum
> 1 cup heavy cream
> 2 tablespoons powdered sugar
> 1 teaspoon vanilla extract

Wash the peaches. Place the water and sugar in a saucepan and boil gently for 5 minutes. Add the peaches and poach in the simmering syrup for 5 minutes. Peel the peaches. Cut each in half. Remove the pits and place in a baking dish, cavity side up. Combine the almonds and sugar cookie crumbs. Mound the mixture into each peach cavity. Sprinkle with sherry or rum. Pour 1/2 cup of the peach cooking syrup into the baking dish. Cover and bake in a preheated 350° oven for 20 minutes.
Beat the cream until it begins to thicken. Add the sugar and vanilla and continue beating until the cream is thick. Serve the hot peaches with whipped cream. The peaches can also be served with a raspberry sauce. Drain a package of frozen raspberries and place the berries in a blender. Add the grated rind and juice of 1 orange and blend to form a purée. Force the purée through a fine strainer to remove the seeds.

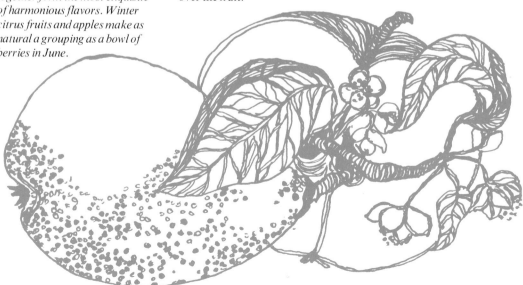

Baked bananas with hot chocolate rum sauce

4 servings

- 4 *large bananas*
- 2 *tablespoons butter*
- 4 *tablespoons brown sugar*
- 4 *teaspoons honey*
- 1 *tablespoon lemon juice*
- $1/2$ *teaspoon cinnamon*
- $1/4$ *teaspoon nutmeg*

Chocolate rum sauce:

- 1 *(6 ounce) package semi-sweet chocolate pieces*
- $1/3$ *cup water*
- 2 *tablespoons butter*
- $1/4$ *cup heavy cream*
- 2 *tablespoons rum*

Peel and cut each banana in half lengthwise. Place in a buttered baking dish. Dot the bananas with butter and sprinkle with brown sugar. Mix together the honey, lemon juice, cinnamon and nutmeg. Pour over the bananas. Cover and bake in a preheated 300° oven for 30 minutes.

Sauce: Melt the chocolate in the water in a small saucepan over very low heat. Stir in the butter, cream and rum. Place the bananas on serving dishes and serve with the hot sauce. A scoop of ice cream can be hidden beneath the chocolate sauce to make an even richer dessert.

Pineapple in caramel sauce

6 servings

- 1 *small pineapple*
- 3 *tablespoons butter*
- 4 *tablespoons sugar Grated rind and juice of 1 orange*
- 2 *tablespoons Kirsch or orange liqueur (opt.)*
- 6 *scoops vanilla ice cream*

Peel and cut the pineapple into thin slices. Remove the cores. Heat the butter in a large skillet and fry the pineapple rings over moderate heat until soft. Increase the heat and sprinkle with half of the sugar. Continue cooking 3 minutes until lightly browned. Turn the pineapple rings. Add the remaining sugar, grated orange rind, juice and liqueur. Flame the liqueur with a lighted match. Place pineapple slices on individual dessert plates and spoon a little of the sauce over each ring. Top with a scoop of ice cream. Canned pineapple can also be used if fresh pineapple is not available.

Blueberry cream puffs

8 servings

- 1 *cup water*
- 1 *tablespoon sugar*
- $1/4$ *teaspoon salt*
- 4 *tablespoons butter, cut into small pieces*
- 1 *cup sifted flour*
- 4 *whole eggs*
- 1 *egg yolk*
- 2 *tablespoons milk*
- $1^1/2$ *cups heavy cream*
- 2 *tablespoons powdered sugar*
- 1 *teaspoon vanilla*
- 1 *cup blueberries*

Place the water, sugar, salt and butter in a saucepan. Adjust the heat so the butter has melted by the moment the water reaches boiling point. Add the flour and beat the mixture over low heat for 3 minutes until a ball of dough is formed. Remove the pan from the heat. Beat in the whole eggs, 1 at a time. Beat well after each addition. Drop the mixture from a tablespoon onto 2 buttered and floured cookie sheets. The puffs will double in bulk as they bake. Combine the egg yolk and and milk with a fork and brush over the mounds. Bake in a preheated 375° oven for 25 minutes until firm and golden. Cool the puffs.

To prepare the filling, whip the cream, adding sugar and vanilla as it begins to thicken. Continue beating until the cream is thick. Fold in the blueberries. Cut each cream puff in half and fill generously with the filling.

Glazed oranges

6 servings

- 6 *beautiful dessert oranges*
- 2 *cups water*
- 2 *cups sugar*
- $1/4$ *teaspoon cream of tartar*
- $1/3$ *cup orange liqueur (optional)*

Remove the thinnest possible strips of peel from 3 oranges and cut into tiny strips about 1 inch long and as thin as possible. Peel the remaining oranges and remove any white pith.

Bring the water, sugar and cream of tartar to boiling point. Add the orange rind and simmer the syrup until reduced to $1^1/2$ cups. Place the oranges in a glass serving bowl. Stir the orange liqueur into the syrup. Pour the hot syrup and rind over the oranges. Cool and chill in the refrigerator for at least 4 hours before serving.

Pick your favorite from this garland of goodies that have gone right to America's sweet tooth for 200 years. Clockwise: Strawberry ice (recipe below), Glazed oranges, Blueberry cream puffs (recipes page 75), Cherries jubilee (recipe page 77), Baked melon Alaska.

Strawberry ice

6 servings

> 1 package unflavored gelatin
> 1/4 cup water
> 2 pints ripe strawberries
> 1 cup milk
> 3/4 cup sugar
> 2 tablespoons orange liqueur (optional)
> 2 egg whites

Sprinkle the gelatin over the water and set aside to soften. Rinse and hull the strawberries and dry them thoroughly. Purée the strawberries in a blender and force through a fine strainer. Combine the milk and sugar in a saucepan. Bring to a simmer, stirring constantly. Add the softened gelatin to the milk mixture and sir until it dissolves. Combine the milk mixture, strawberry purée and the optional orange liqueur. Pour into an 8 × 8 × 2 inch pan and freeze until mushy. Transfer the ice to a mixing bowl. Add the egg whites and beat with an electric mixer a few minutes. Return the ice to the square pan and freeze until firm.

Baked melon Alaska

6 servings

> 3 small cantaloupe melons
> 6 tablespoons brandy
> 5 egg whites
> 1/4 teaspoon salt
> 1/8 teaspoon cream of tartar
> 1 teaspoon vanilla
> 1 1/4 cups sugar
> 6 scoops vanilla ice cream

Cut melons in half horizontally. Discard the seeds and form the melon into balls with a melon scoop. Leave the melon balls inside shells. Add 1 tablespoon brandy or fruit juice to each half. To prepare the meringue, place the egg whites, salt, cream of tartar and vanilla in a large bowl. Beat until the egg whites stand in soft peaks. Add sugar gradually and continue beating until stiff and shiny. Place a generous scoop of ice cream in each melon half. Spoon meringue over the ice cream to enclose it completely. Place in 2 baking dishes and surround the melon shells with ice. Bake in a preheated 475° oven for 3 to 4 minutes until the meringue is delicately browned. Serve immediately.

At circuses, Halloween and county fairs, children's eyes grow as big and round as candied apples. Recipe tells how to make them at home in ten minutes.

Candied apples

6 servings

    6 *large red apples*
    2 *cups sugar*
  $^1/_2$ *cup light corn syrup*
  $^3/_4$ *cup water*
    2 *teaspoons vinegar*
      Red vegetable coloring
    3 *tablespoons butter*
      Few drops oil of cinnamon
      (optional)

Wash the apples, dry thoroughly and insert a wooden skewer into the stem end of each. Combine the sugar, corn syrup, water and vinegar in a small deep saucepan. Cook slowly, stirring constantly, until the sugar is dissolved. Add enough coloring to color deep red. Add the butter and stir to dissolve. Boil the mixture until it reaches the hard crack stage or 290° on a candy thermometer. Remove from heat. Add oil of cinnamon, stirring only enough to mix. Place the saucepan over boiling water. Dip the apples, 1 at a time, in the syrup, twisting as the apple is removed. Place on a well oiled cookie sheet to cool and harden.

Cherries jubilee

6 servings

    2 *pounds fresh or canned*
      black Bing cherries,
      pitted
      Grated rind and juice of
      1 orange
    2 *tablespoons red currant*
      jelly
    1 *teaspoon cinnamon*
    1 *tablespoon cornstarch,*
      dissolved in
  $^3/_4$ *cup cherry juice*
      or orange juice
  $^1/_4$ *cup brandy, warmed*
    6 *scoops vanilla ice cream*

Place the cherries in a heavy saucepan. Add grated orange rind, orange juice, red currant jelly and cinnamon. Cover and cook over low heat for 10 minutes, or until cherries have softened if fresh cherries are used. Cook 5 minutes if using canned cherries. Stir in cornstarch dissolved in cold juice. Continue cooking until a thick sauce has formed. Light the brandy and pour the flames slowly over the cherries. Spoon the hot cherries over vanilla ice cream and serve immediately.

Breads

At one time bakers were not allowed to leave their trade and their children were not permitted to marry outside the profession. Bakers were exempted from military service but, there is always a catch to every privilege, they were forced to live up to their obligations to the community. If the quality of the bread was poor, the baker ran the risk of either being baked in his own oven or enduring the public humiliation of walking through the streets with the miserable, unacceptable loaf tied around his neck. To guard against the possible accusation of selling short weight, the bakers proclaimed their honesty by throwing in an extra loaf for each batch of twelve. This form of insurance is known as a 'baker's dozen.'

In early colonial times, few private citizens owned their own oven. Instead, the food was cooked in an open fireplace. The Sabbath was observed from sundown on Saturday until sundown on Sunday, thus making it impossible for the devout Pilgrims to watch the fire continuously. Instead, the local baker would pick up the family pot of beans, bake it slowly in his oven and return it on Sunday with a loaf of his own brown bread.

Pancakes

6 servings

> 2 cups sifted flour
> 1 teaspoon salt
> 1 tablespoon sugar
> 2 teaspoons baking powder
> 2 eggs, lightly beaten
> 1 1/2 cups milk
> 2 tablespoons butter, melted
> 2 tablespoons oil
> 1/2 cup butter
> Maple syrup

Sift the flour, salt, sugar and baking powder into a mixing bowl. Add the eggs, milk and melted butter. Stir until the ingredients are just mixed. Do not overmix or the pancakes will be heavy. Heat 1 tablespoon oil in a large skillet. Add enough batter to form 4 separate pancakes. When bubbles appear in the surface, lift a corner of each pancake and see if it is well browned on the underside. Turn the pancakes and cook on the second side for about 3 minutes. Continue until all the pancake batter is used, adding a little oil to the skillet to prevent them from sticking. Serve pancakes with butter and maple syrup. **Note:** If you are making a large batch of pancakes, place them in a single layer on a cookie sheet lined with a tea towel and keep them warm in a 200° oven. Do not stack the pancakes on top of each other or they will steam, become soggy and stick together.

Biscuits

16 biscuits

> 2 cups sifted all purpose flour
> 4 teaspoons baking powder
> 1/2 teaspoon salt
> 1/4 cup shortening
> 1/4 cup butter
> 2/3 cup milk

Sift the flour, baking powder and salt together into a bowl. Cut the shortening and butter into the flour with a pastry blender or 2 knives until the mixture resembles coarse meal. Add the milk and stir with a fork. Gather the dough into a ball, and knead on a lightly floured board 30 to 45 seconds. Pat or roll the dough to a 1/2 inch thickness. Dip a 2 inch biscuit cutter into flour and cut as many biscuits as possible. Knead the scraps into a ball, roll out the dough again and cut as many more biscuits as possible. Place the biscuits in an ungreased 9 × 9 × 2 inch baking pan and bake in a 450° oven 12 to 15 minutes until golden brown. Serve immediately.

Popovers

Makes 12 popovers

> 1 cup flour
> 1/4 teaspoon salt
> 1 cup milk
> 2 eggs
> 1 tablespoon oil

Preheat the oven to 450°. Lightly grease the muffin pans and place in the oven to heat.
Sift the flour and measure 1 cup. Place the flour in a blender and add the remaining ingredients. Blend until smooth. Fill the muffin pans 1/2 full with the batter. Bake for 30 minutes until the popovers have risen and are firm and lightly browned.
Serve popovers with butter and preserves, with bacon and eggs or roast beef.

If you find you have to leave the house before the bread has completely risen, put the dough in the refrigerator. It will rise more slowly but will not come to any harm.

White bread

1 cup lukewarm water
1 package dry yeast
1 cup milk
4 tablespoons butter
1 tablespoon sugar
1 teaspoon salt
6 cups unbleached white flour
1 egg yolk
$^1/_4$ cup milk

Pour the water into a large bowl. Add yeast and stir to dissolve. Heat the milk to simmering point. Remove from heat. Stir the butter, sugar and salt into the hot milk. and cool until lukewarm. Stir milk mixture into the yeast and water. Add the flour gradually until the dough pulls away from the sides of the bowl. Turn the dough onto a floured board. Knead for 15 minutes until the dough is smooth and elastic. Place the dough in an oiled bowl, turning it once to oil the entire surface of the dough. Cover with a damp towel and leave it to rise until doubled in bulk. Punch the dough down several times to allow the air to escape. Cut it in half and knead each piece into a smooth dough. Shape into 2 loaves, 2 balls or several rolls and place in oiled loaf pans or on cookie sheets. Cover and leave 1 more hour until again doubled in bulk. Combine the egg yolk and milk with a fork and brush on the dough. Bake in the center of a preheated 375° oven for 1 hour. Remove from the pans and cool on wire racks.

Boston brown bread

$^1/_2$ cup yellow cornmeal
$^1/_2$ cup rye flour
$^1/_2$ cup graham flour
1 teaspoon baking soda
$^1/_2$ teaspoon salt
$^3/_4$ cup milk
2 tablespoons butter, melted
6 tablespoons molasses
$^1/_2$ cup currants

Sift the cornmeal, rye flour, graham flour, baking soda and salt into a bowl. Combine the milk, butter, molasses and currants in a separate bowl and stir into the dry ingredients. Pour the batter into a buttered 4 cup bowl. Steam over simmering water for $1^1/_2$ to 2 hours or until a cake tester inserted in the center comes out clean. Boston brown bread is traditionally served with Boston baked beans.

Whole wheat bread

3 cups lukewarm water
1 package dry yeast
$^1/_4$ cup honey
1 cup dry milk
7 to 8 cups whole wheat flour
4 teaspoons salt
4 tablespoons butter, melted
1 egg yolk
$^1/_4$ cup milk

Measure the water into a large bowl. Add the yeast and stir until the yeast has dissolved. Stir in the honey and dry milk. Add $3^1/_2$ cups flour, 1 cup at a time. Beat with a wooden spoon or spatula until a smooth batter is formed. Cover the bowl with a damp cloth and leave for 1 hour until doubled in bulk. Stir the salt and melted butter into the 'sponge.' Fold in the remaining flour. Add a little more flour if the dough appears sticky. Turn the dough onto a floured board and knead for at least 10 minutes until the dough is smooth and elastic. This is fairly hard work at the beginning as the dough is quite firm. Replace the dough in the oiled bowl. Cover and leave for another hour until doubled in bulk. Punch the dough down several times and knead for 5 minutes. Cover and leave the dough to rise again for 1 hour. Divide the dough into 3 equal pieces. Let it rest for 5 minutes and then shape into 3 loaves. Place the loaves in oiled loaf pans or on cookie sheets. Cover again and allow it to rise for a final hour until again doubled in bulk.

Combine the egg yolk and milk with a fork and brush over the loaves. Bake in the center of a preheated 350° oven for 1 hour. Remove the loaves and cool them on wire racks. You will now be the most popular person in your house.

What is it that makes homemade bread so special? The magic of rising dough, the fragrant joy that fills the house when the loaves come out of the oven? The old-fashioned solid satisfaction of its taste? Clockwise: White bread (recipe page 79), Popovers (recipe page 78). Whole wheat bread (recipe page 79), Corn bread, and Biscuits (recipe page 78).

Corn bread

6 servings

    1 *cup sifted flour*
    1 *cup yellow cornmeal*
    1 *teaspoon salt*
    2 *tablespoons sugar*
    4 *teaspoons baking powder*
    1 *cup milk*
    1 *egg, lightly beaten*
    4 *tablespoons butter, melted*

Sift the flour, cornmeal, salt, sugar and baking powder into a bowl. Add the milk, egg and melted butter. Stir lightly until the ingredients are just combined. Spread into a buttered 9 inch square baking dish. Bake in a preheated 425° oven for 25 minutes. Cut into squares and serve hot.
Corn bread can be served for breakfast with butter and honey or for dinner with fried chicken.

Special occasions

Throughout the year special occasions are celebrated with special foods. A Christmas Dinner to wrap up a happy day: Wine consomme (recipe page 92), Roast beef (recipe page 92),

Glazed baby carrots (recipe page 94), Brussels sprouts with chestnuts (recipe page 93). Baked stuffed potatoes, Coconut cake and tiny Mincemeat pies (recipe page 94).

Easter

Easter wakens the sleeping earth and flowers dance into bloom. Trees, freshly green, bend with the soft breezes of spring. The Easter bunny, one of the most prolific of all animals, brings sugar candy and chocolate eggs to the children as symbols of birth and rebirth. There are hot cross buns for breakfast and a new outfit for the new life just beginning. There is an Easter parade to display the fine feathers and Easter egg hunts are organized to find baskets full of painted and decorated eggs. Baby lamb, innocent and tender, is served for dinner, with fresh young peas and with potatoes so new they can be cooked in their jackets. The lemon meringue pie is as puffy as a cloud and disappears in a fleeting moment.

Stuffed eggs with smoked salmon

6 servings

> 6 hard boiled eggs
> 1 (3 ounce) package Philadelphia cream cheese
> 1/4 cup mayonnaise
> 1 teaspoon lemon juice
> 1/4 pound smoked salmon
>   Freshly ground black pepper
> 1 bunch watercress

Cut the eggs in half lengthwise. Scoop out the yolks and force them through a fine strainer. Beat the cheese until softened and stir in the egg yolks, mayonnaise and lemon juice. Shred the salmon into thin strips. Fold half of the salmon into the cream cheese mixture. Fill the egg whites with the mixture. Scatter the remaining salmon over the eggs. Dust with black pepper. Garnish with watercress.

Rack of lamb

6 servings

> 1 rack of lamb
> 3 tablespoons butter, melted
> 2 tablespoons finely chopped parsley
> 1 tablespoon chervil (optional)
> 1 teaspoon thyme
> 2 tablespoons finely chopped chives
> 1/2 cup freshly made bread crumbs
> 1 teaspoon salt
>   Freshly ground black pepper

Brush the lamb with part of the melted butter. Place on a roasting rack and roast, uncovered, in a preheated 425° oven for 15 minutes. Remove from the heat and press the combined herbs, bread crumbs, salt and pepper over the meat. Brush with the remaining melted butter and continue cooking, uncovered in a 375° oven for 15

Mint sauce

6 servings

> 1/2 cup fresh mint leaves
> 1/2 teaspoon salt
> 1 teaspoon sugar
> 1/2 cup vinegar
> 2 tablespoons water

Chop the mint leaves with the salt and sugar. Place in a sauceboat and add the vinegar and water. Allow the sauce to stand for 1 hour before serving.

Lemon meringue pie

6 servings

Filling:

$1^1/_2$ *cups sugar*
  $^1/_4$ *teaspoon salt*
   6 *tablespoons cornstarch*
   2 *cups boiling water*
   4 *egg yolks, lightly beaten*
  $^2/_3$ *cup lemon juice*
   1 *tablespoon grated lemon rind*
   2 *teaspoons butter*
  $^1/_2$ *recipe pastry (see Apple pie recipe page 68)*

Meringue:

   5 *egg whites*
  $^1/_8$ *teaspoon cream of tartar*
      Pinch of salt
   6 *tablespoons sugar*

Sift the sugar, salt and cornstarch together into a saucepan. Add the boiling water gradually, stirring constantly with a wire whisk. Cook over very low heat, stirring until the mixture is thick. Remove from the heat and stir in the egg yolks, lemon juice and lemon rind. Return to the heat and cook, stirring constantly, 1 to 2 minutes until very thick. Do not allow the mixture to boil. Remove from the heat and stir in the butter until melted. Cool the mixture completely. Meanwhile roll out the pastry and fit it into a deep 9 inch pie plate. Prick the bottom with a fork. Fit a sheet of aluminium foil firmly over the pastry and weight it with rice or dried beans. Bake in a 400° oven 8 minutes. Remove the foil and bake 4 minutes more until brown.

Spoon the lemon mixture into the baked pie shell. Beat the egg whites with the cream of tartar and salt until soft peaks form. Add the sugar and beat until stiff. Spoon the meringue on top of the filling, spreading it to seal the edges. Make peaks in the meringue with the back of a spoon. Bake in a 300° oven about 30 minutes or until the meringue is delicately browned. Cool before serving.

84

An Easter feast as delicate and full of promise as the first flowers of spring: Stuffed eggs with smoked salmon, Rack of lamb, Mint sauce (recipes page 82), June peas and new potatoes.

July 4th

An easy-to-make celebration of Independence Day: Charcoal broiled sirloin steak, Broiled tomatoes (recipes page 86), Tossed salad, Strawberry ice cream (recipes page 87).

1976 marks the 200th anniversary of America's Declaration of Independence and every year this act of defiance is celebrated with all the joy of a midsummer holiday. The 4th of July means picnics, shimmering hot beaches, ball games, political speeches, parades, cookouts and firecrackers.
The food is simple but plentiful. There are hot dogs and hamburgers, steaks and baked potatoes. The tomatoes are bursting with red ripe flavor and the corn is as sweet as the morning dew. Freshly churned ice cream, rich, creamy and brimming with strawberries, is almost sinfully delicious. There is iced tea and plenty of beer and always a watermelon, just in case anybody is still hungry.

Shrimp in beer batter

6 servings

Batter:
$^3/_4$ *cup beer*
$^3/_4$ *cup flour*
$^1/_2$ *teaspoon salt*
   Freshly ground black
   pepper
 1 *teaspoon paprika*

24 *large shrimp*
   Juice of 1 lemon
$^1/_2$ *cup flour*
   Oil or shortening for deep
   frying

Place the batter ingredients in a bowl and stir with a wire whisk until smooth.
Peel and devein the shrimp. Cut shrimp into a fantail, leaving the tail shell intact. Sprinkle shrimp with lemon juice. Dip in flour and then into batter.
Deep fry shrimp in hot oil for 4 minutes. Remove and drain the shrimp. Heat the oil again until it is very hot. Plunge shrimp into hot oil and continue cooking for 2 minutes until crisp and golden. Drain and serve immediately.
As you can see, this batter does not contain any eggs so it is crisp, delicious and as light as a cloud. It can also be used as a batter for other fish such as trout or oysters.

Stuffed sirloin steak

4 servings

 4 *(1 inch thick) individual*
   steaks or
 1 *large steak*
 2 *tablespoons butter*
 1 *onion, finely chopped*
 8 *small mushrooms, finely*
   chopped
 2 *slices boiled ham, diced*
 1 *teaspoon lemon juice*
 2 *tablespoons finely*
   chopped parsley
$^1/_2$ *teaspoon thyme*
 1 *teaspoon salt*
   Freshly ground black
   pepper
 1 *tablespoon oil*

Cut the steak almost in half lengthwise to form a pocket for the filling. Heat the butter in a skillet and fry the onion for 3 minutes until softened. Add the mushrooms and cook over moderate heat for 5 minutes. Remove from the heat and stir in all the remaining ingredients except the oil.
Sandwich the stuffing into the cavity in the steak. Sew the 2 sides together with string or secure with toothpicks. Brush the steak on both sides with oil. Broil under the broiler or over charcoal 5 minutes on each side.

Broiled tomatoes

6 servings

 6 *medium sized tomatoes*
$^1/_2$ *cup freshly made*
   breadcrumbs
 3 *tablespoons finely*
   chopped parsley
 2 *tablespoons chopped*
   chives
 1 *teaspoon basil*
 1 *teaspoon salt*
   Freshly ground black
   pepper
 6 *teaspoons butter*

Cut each tomato in half and place on a cookie sheet. Combine the breadcrumbs with all the remaining ingredients except the butter. Press a small mound of the breadcrumb mixture on top of each tomato half and dot with a teaspoon of butter. Bake the tomatoes in a preheated 350° oven for 15 minutes. Remove from the oven and place under a preheated broiler for 3 minutes until the breadcrumbs are lightly browned.

Tossed salad

Strawberry ice cream

6 servings

1 head curly endive lettuce
1 head Romaine lettuce or
 any other crisp, fresh lettuce
$1/2$ Bermuda onion, very
 thinly sliced
2 ripe tomatoes, cut into
 wedges
1 avocado, peeled and sliced
1 tablespoon lemon juice
1 cucumber, peeled and sliced
1 cup mayonnaise
2 tablespoons sour cream
$1/4$ cup blue cheese
2 tablespoons vinegar
1 teaspoon oregano,
 marjoram or dill weed

Cut the lettuce into bite sized
pieces. Wash and dry
thoroughly. Place in a large
bowl. Add the Bermuda onion
and tomatoes. Slice the avocado
and sprinkle with lemon juice to
prevent discoloration. Add
avocado and cucumber slices to
the salad bowl. Combine the
mayonnaise, sour cream, blue
cheese, vinegar and 1 of the
herbs. Toss the salad with the
dressing.

5 egg yolks
1 cup sugar
1 cup milk or
 light cream
1 cup heavy
 cream
2 teaspoons vanilla
1 quart strawberries

Beat the egg yolks and sugar
together until very thick. Stir in
the milk and pour the mixture
into a heavy saucepan or the top
of a double boiler. Cook over
low heat, stirring constantly
until thickened into a light
custard. Remove from the heat
and cool the custard. Beat the
cream with the vanilla
until lightly whipped and about
the same consistency as the
custard. Fold the cream into the
custard. Slice the strawberries
and force them through a fine
strainer to remove the seeds.
Fold the strawberry purée into
the custard cream. Churn the
mixture in an ice cream churn
until thickened. Freeze for 2
hours until firm.

Thanksgiving

A traditional Thanksgiving menu that Captain John Smith and Pocahontas might have shared: Roast turkey, Onions in cream sauce, Sweet potatoes, Mashed potatoes (recipe page 90), Cranberries and Pumpkin pie (recipes page 91).

Roast turkey

Thanksgiving dinner has remained essentially unchanged since the Pilgrims first joined hands with the Indians to celebrate their victory over hunger and adversity. All the foods for the feast are native to America. Cold oysters, freshly harvested from the chilly New England waters, are served on the half shell. The turkey is borne triumphantly to the table and carved by the master of the house. Nuts, gathered in the fall, give an interesting texture to the sausage stuffing, and the giblet gravy is passed from plate to plate. Cranberries ripened in Massachusetts' sandy soil lend a touch of sweetness, and the mashed potatoes and sweet potatoes, swirling in butter, send steaming clouds of warmth along the length of the table. The acorn squash is baked with a sauce made from autumn ripe apples and onions in cream sauce complete the main course.

For dessert, tradition demands a pumpkin pie, topped with whipped cream, or an apple pie hot from the oven. There is cider for the children and a glass or two of wine for the parents and grandparents, aunts, uncles, cousins and visiting friends.

12 servings

14 pound turkey

Dressing:
- 4 tablespoons butter
- 2 onions, finely chopped
- 2 cups chopped pecans
  Liver from turkey, chopped
- 1 pound sausage meat
- 4 cups freshly made breadcrumbs
- 1 teaspoon salt
  Freshly ground black pepper
- 4 tablespoons finely chopped parsley
- 1 teaspoon sage
- 1 teaspoon thyme
- 2 eggs, lightly beaten
- 3 tablespoons butter, softened or
  3 tablespoons solid shortening
- 1 teaspoon salt
  Freshly ground black pepper
- 1 teaspoon paprika

To prepare the dressing, heat the butter in a large skillet. Sauté the onions and pecans for 5 minutes. Add the turkey liver and fry for 3 minutes. Add sausage meat and continue cooking for 10 minutes until all the fat has rendered. Pour off the fat and remove the skillet from the heat. Stir in the remaining dressing ingredients. Fill the turkey cavity with dressing. Truss the turkey or secure with poultry lacers. Rub the turkey skin with softened butter. Season with salt and pepper and sprinkle with paprika. Place the turkey, breast side up, on a roasting rack and roast, uncovered, in a preheated 350° oven for 4 hours. Test the turkey for doneness by inserting the point of a small knife into the leg. Remove the turkey from the oven. Cover with aluminum foil and allow it to rest for 30 minutes.

Note: The turkey continues to cook from its own internal heat for at least 10 minutes after it has been taken from the oven. If you test the turkey every 10 minutes after the first 4 hours, you will be sure it does not become overcooked and dry. If the juices are clear, without any tinge of pink and the leg moves freely, the turkey is done.

Onions in cream sauce

4 servings

- 2 pounds small white onions, peeled
- 3 tablespoons butter
- 1 teaspoon sugar
- 2 tablespoons flour
- 1 cup milk
- $^{1}/_{2}$ cup heavy cream
- $^{1}/_{2}$ teaspoon salt
  Freshly ground black pepper
- 1 tablespoon lemon juice
- 2 tablespoons finely chopped parsley

Boil the onions in salted water for 10 minutes until slightly softened. Drain the onions. Melt the butter in a skillet. Add the onions and sprinkle with sugar. Fry over low heat for 10 minutes until lightly browned. Stir in the flour and add the milk and cream. Season with salt and pepper. Cover and simmer over low heat for another 10 minutes until the onions are tender and the sauce is rich and creamy. Add lemon juice and garnish with parsley.
These onions are very good with boiled beef, roast chicken or turkey.

Baked potatoes

4 servings

- 4 uniformly sized Idaho baking potatoes
- 4 tablespoons butter
- 4 tablespoons milk or heavy cream
- 1 teaspoon salt
  Freshly ground black pepper
- 1 teaspoon chervil or marjoram
- $^{1}/_{3}$ cup grated Swiss cheese
- $^{1}/_{3}$ cup grated Parmesan cheese

Scrub the potatoes, prick with fork and wrap in aluminium foil. Bake on a cookie sheet in a preheated 350° oven for $1^{1}/_{4}$ hours until soft. Cut each potato in half lengthwise. Scoop out the potato and reserve the shells. Mash the hot potato in a bowl adding 3 tablespoons butter, milk, salt, pepper and chervil. Fill the mixture into the potato shells. Sprinkle with the combined grated cheeses and dot with the remaining butter. Place in a hot 425° oven for 10 minutes until the cheese has melted and a golden crust has formed.
The potatoes can be prepared in advance and reheated in a 350° oven for 25 minutes.

Mashed potatoes

6 servings

- 6 medium sized baking potatoes
- 3 tablespoons butter
- $^{1}/_{2}$ cup milk or cream
  salt to taste
  Freshly ground black pepper

Peel the potatoes and cut into small pieces. Boil potatoes in salted water for 20 minutes until tender. Drain and mash the potatoes, adding butter and milk. Mash until smooth and season with salt and pepper. To keep the potatoes warm, transfer them to a buttered baking dish. Dot with more butter.

Giblet gravy

Turkey giblets (except the
   livers)
1 onion, chopped
1 carrot, chopped
1 stalk celery, sliced
4 cups chicken broth
2 sprigs parsley
1 bay leaf
2 tablespoons butter
3 tablespoons flour
$^1/_2$ teaspoon salt
   Freshly ground black
   pepper

Place the turkey giblets, onion,
carrot, celery, chicken broth,
parsley sprigs and bay leaf in a
saucepan. Cover and simmer
over low heat for 2 hours. Strain
the broth.
Heat the butter in a clean
saucepan. Stir in the flour and
add the strained broth gradually,
stirring with a wire whisk.
Season with salt and pepper and
serve very hot.

Cranberry sauce

4 cups (1 pound) cranberries
2 cups water
2 cups sugar
   Grated rind of 1 orange
2 tablespoons brandy
   (optional)

Wash the cranberries and
discard any unripe berries. Place
the water and sugar in a
saucepan and boil for 10 minutes
to form a syrup. Add cranberries
and boil for 5 minutes or until
berries begin to pop. Remove
from the heat and add orange
rind and brandy. Chill the sauce
for 4 hours before serving.

Pumpkin pie

Use $^1/_2$ pastry recipe
   from Apple pie
   (recipe on page 68)
2 cups mashed pumpkin,
   freshly cooked or canned
$^1/_2$ cup brown sugar
2 eggs, lightly beaten
1 cup milk
1 cup heavy cream
$^1/_2$ teaspoon powdered ginger
1 teaspoon cinnamon
$^1/_4$ teaspoon salt
$^1/_4$ cup brandy (optional)

Mash the pumpkin in a bowl and
stir in the remaining ingredients
until smooth.
Line a 9 inch pie plate with
pastry. Pour the filling into the
unbaked shell. Bake in a 350°
oven for 50 minutes or until a
toothpick inserted into the center
of the filling comes out clean.
Chill the pie and serve with
sweetened whipped cream. Dust
the cream with cinnamon.

Christmas

Christmas dinner shines like a jewel in the middle of the long dark winter. The preparations begin weeks in advance. Fragrant spicy breads are baked and cookies are decorated to hang on the Christmas tree, or for giving to friends and neighbors. Della Robia wreaths, made from evergreen boughs, nuts, apples and scarlet ribbons are hung on the front door, and every surface inside the house reveals a Christmas ornament.

Friends and relatives travel across the country to be together at Christmas time and join in the celebrations.

Dinner is served.

A light clear soup anticipates the majestic prime ribs of beef. Baked potatoes wear jackets of silver foil. Brussels sprouts are partnered with shiny glazed carrots.

Some families, particularly those with ties to England, still serve their own homemade Christmas pudding for dessert. This is perhaps the most symbolic of all foods. Before it is cooked, every member of the family stirs the pudding in a clockwise direction, corresponding with the way the sun was once thought to revolve around the earth. (To stir the wrong way forecasts a year of troubles.) The pudding is then put into a bowl and steamed until it becomes a firm, round 'world' of goodness. A sprig of holly crowns the pudding with its red berries representing the blood of Christ. Satanic flames of brandy are poured over the 'world' and they lick greedily beneath and over the 'earth'. But happily they soon fade away and once again goodness triumphs over evil! The pudding, like life itself, contains all sorts of surprises. The touch of bitter lemon peel is almost lost in the happiness of the sweet meats and silver charms.

After the Christmas pudding there is a choice between mincemeat pies, a snowy white coconut cake or a long nap in front of the fire.

Wine consommé

8 servings

> 3 pounds soup bones with beef clinging to the bones
> 2 pounds brisket of beef
> 1 onion, chopped
> 3 stalks celery, chopped
> 3 sprigs parsley
> 2 bay leaves
> 1 teaspoon peppercorns
> 1 teaspoon thyme
> 8 cups cold water
> 2 cups red wine
> 1 teaspoon salt
> Freshly ground black pepper
> $1/2$ cup finely chopped chives

Place the soup bones, brisket, onion, celery, parsley, bay leaves, peppercorns and thyme in a large soup pot. Cover with cold water. Place the lid $1/3$ of the way over the pot to allow some evaporation. Simmer for 4 hours. Strain the broth and chill it in the refrigerator. Remove the fat which will rise to the surface. Simmer the broth until it has reduced to 5 cups and add the wine. Season with salt and pepper. Garnish with chopped chives. Serve hot or cold.

Roast beef

8 servings

> 8 ribs of beef
> 2 teaspoons salt
> Freshly ground black pepper

Stand the beef, fat side up, in a roasting pan. Season with salt and pepper. Insert a meat thermometer into the center of the meat, making sure the tip does not touch the bone. Roast the beef, uncovered, in a 450° oven for 15 minutes. Reduce the heat to 350° and continue cooking, allowing a total cooking time of 18 minutes to the pound for rare beef (internal meat thermometer reading 130°). Allow 22 minutes to the pound for medium beef (internal temperature 150°). Allow 28 to 30 minutes to the pound for well done beef (internal temperature 165°).

Remove the beef from the oven. Cover with aluminum foil and let it stand for 15 minutes to allow the juices to return to the center of the beef.

Brussels sprouts with chestnuts

8 servings

> 2 pints Brussels sprouts
> $^1/_4$ cup water
> $^1/_2$ teaspoon salt
>   1 (1 pound) can chestnuts or
>   2 pounds fresh chestnuts,
>   boiled for 30 minutes and
>   peeled
> 2 tablespoons butter
>   Freshly ground black
>   pepper

Wash sprouts and discard outer leaves. Cut a cross in the base of each sprout to speed the cooking process. Place sprouts in a saucepan. Add water and salt. Cover and steam sprouts over low heat for 10 minutes. Add chestnuts and continue steaming for 5 or 6 minutes until chestnuts are hot and sprouts are tender. Toss with butter and season with pepper.

Baked sweet potatoes

6 servings

> 6 medium sized sweet
>   potatoes
> 3 tablespoons butter,
>   softened

Scrub the potato skins until they are clean. Prick with fork. Rub the skins with butter and wrap in aluminum foil. Place on a baking sheet and bake the potatoes in a preheated 350° oven for 1 hour until tender.

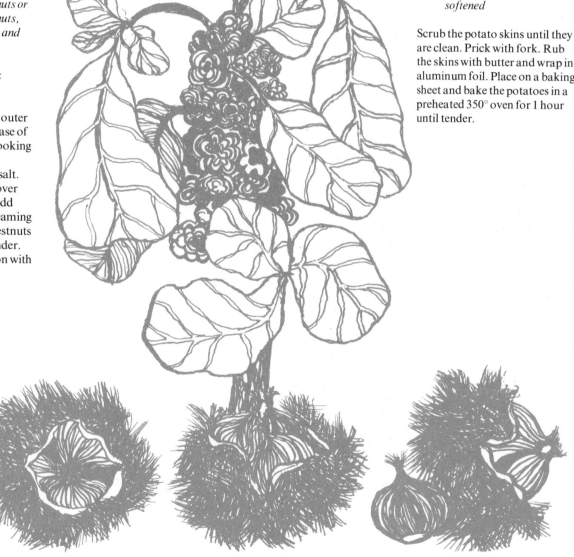

Glazed baby carrots

Mincemeat pie

8 servings

- 40 *baby carrots or*
  2 pounds long young
  carrots
- $^1/_2$ *teaspoon salt*
- 2 *cups water*
- 2 *tablespoons butter*
- 2 *teaspoons sugar*
- $^1/_4$ *cup white vermouth or*
  chicken broth
- 2 *tablespoons finely*
  chopped parsley

Peel the carrots and slice the long carrots. Simmer for 15 minutes in salted water and drain. Melt the butter in a skillet. Add the parboiled carrots and sprinkle with sugar. Cook over moderate heat for 5 minutes. Add the vermouth and cook for another 5 minutes until the vermouth has evaporated and the carrots are tender and shiny. Garnish with finely chopped parsley. If you prepare the carrots in advance, reheat them in a buttered baking dish. Cover them with foil and place them in a preheated 350° oven for 10 minutes. Add the parsley garnish at the last minute.

Pastry:
- $2^1/_2$ *cups sifted all purpose flour*
- $^1/_4$ *teaspoon salt*
- 6 *tablespoons butter*
- 6 *tablespoons solid*
  shortening or margarine
- 8 *tablespoons cold water*

Filling:
- 4 *cups mincemeat*

Glaze:
- 1 *egg yolk*
- 2 *tablespoons milk*
- $^1/_4$ *cup powdered sugar*

To prepare the pastry, place the sifted flour and salt in a bowl. Cut the butter into small pieces and mix with the flour, using a pastry blender or your fingertips. When the butter is about the size of small peas, mix in shortening in the same way. Stir in enough water with a fork to form the dough into a ball. Wrap in waxed paper and chill for 20 minutes. Cut the pastry into 2 unequal halves. Roll into circles on a floured board. To assemble the pie, fit the larger circle into a 9 inch pie plate. Cover with mincemeat. Top with the second round of pastry. Make a design of small cuts in the top of the pastry to allow the steam to escape. Combine the egg yolk and milk with a fork and brush onto the pastry. Bake in a preheated 375° oven for 45 minutes. Dust with sifted powdered sugar. The mincemeat pies can also be baked in muffin tins, cutting circles of pastry with a cookie cutter. Serve hot, with grilled tomatoes and a tossed green salad.

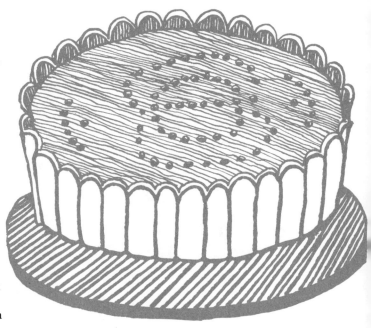

Kitchen terms

Aspic
A stiff gelatin obtained by combining fish or meat bouillon with gelatin powder.

Au gratin
Obtained by covering a dish with a white sauce (usually prepared with grated cheese) and then heating the dish in the oven so that a golden crust forms.

Baste
To moisten meat or other foods while cooking to add flavor and to prevent drying of the surface. The liquid is usually melted fat, meat drippings, fruit juice or sauce.

Blanch (precook)
To preheat in boiling water or steam. (1) Used to inactivate enzymes and shrink food for canning, freezing, and drying. Vegetables are blanched in boiling water or steam, and fruits in boiling fruit juice, syrup, water, or steam. (2) Used to aid in removal of skins from nuts, fruits, and some vegetables.

Blend
To mix thoroughly two or more ingredients.

Bouillon
Brown stock, conveniently made by dissolving a bouillon cube in water.

Broth
Water in which meat, fish or vegetables have been boiled or cooked.

'En papillote'
Meat, fish or vegetables wrapped in grease-proof paper or aluminum foil (usually first sprinkled with oil or butter, herbs and seasonings) and then baked in the oven or grilled over charcoal. Most of the taste and aroma are preserved in this way.

Fold
To combine by using two motions, cutting vertically through the mixture and turning over and over by sliding the implement across the bottom of the mixing bowl with each turn.

Fry
To cook in fat; applied especially (1) to cooking in a small amount of fat, also called sauté or pan-fry; (2) to cooking in a deep layer of fat, also called deep-fat frying.

Marinate
To let food stand in a marinade, usually an oil–acid mixture like French dressing.

Parboil
To boil until partially cooked. The cooking is usually completed by another method.

Poach
To cook in a hot liquid using precautions to retain shape. The temperature used varies with the food.

Reduce
To concentrate the taste and aroma of a particular liquid or food e.g. wine, bouillon, soup, sauce etc. by boiling in a pan with the lid off so that the excess water can evaporate.

Roast
To cook, uncovered, by dry heat. Usually done in an oven, but occasionally in ashes, under coals or on heated stones or metals. The term is usually applied to meats but may refer to other food as potatoes, corn, chestnuts.

Sauté
To brown or cook in a small amount of fat. See Fry.

Simmer
To cook in a liquid just below the boiling point, at temperatures of 185°–210°. Bubbles form slowly and collapse below the surface.

Skim
To take away a layer of fat from soup, sauces, etc.

Stock
The liquid in which meat or fish has been boiled together with herbs and vegetables.

Whip
To beat rapidly to produce expansion due to incorporation of air, as applied to cream, eggs, and gelatin dishes.

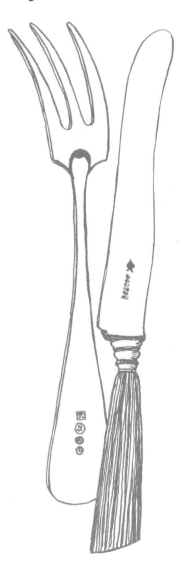

Conversion tables

Liquid measures

American standard cup		metric equivalent (approximately)
1 cup = ½ pint	= 8 fl. oz. (fluid ounce)	= 2,37 dl (deciliter)
1 tbs. (tablespoon) = ½ fl. oz.		= 1,5 cl (centiliter)
1 tsp. (teaspoon) = ⅙ fl. oz.		= 0,5 cl
1 pint	= 16 fl. oz.	= 4,73 dl
1 quart = 2 pints	= 32 fl. oz.	= 9,46 dl

British standard cup		metric equivalent (approximately)
1 cup = ½ pint	= 10 fl. oz.	= 2,84 dl
1 tbs.	= 0.55 fl. oz.	= 1,7 cl
1 tsp.	= ⅕ fl. oz.	= 0,6 cl
1 pint	= 20 fl. oz.	= 5,7 dl
1 quart = 2 pints	= 40 fl. oz.	= 1,1 l (liter)

1 cup = 16 tablespoons
1 tablespoon = 3 teaspoons

1 liter = 10 deciliter = 100 centiliter

Oven temperatures

Centigrade	Fahrenheit	
up to 105° C	up to 225° F	cool
105–135° C	225–275° F	very slow
135–160° C	275–325° F	slow
175–190° C	350–375° F	moderate
215–230° C	400–450° F	hot
230–260° C	450–500° F	very hot
260° C	500° F	extremely hot

Solid measures

American/British		metric equivalent (approximately)
1 lb. (pound)	= 16 oz. (ounces)	= 453 g (gram)
	1 oz.	= 28 g
2.2 lbs.		= 1000 g = 1 kg (kilogram)
	3½ oz.	= 100 g

Alphabetical index

Index by type of dish

Photo credits:

Photo p. 4 (top)	American Hereford Association
Photo p. 4 (below)	International Harvester Company
Photo p. 5 (top)	Department of Sea and Fisheries, Augusta, Maine
Photo p. 8 (top left)	Progressive Grocer Magazine
Photo p. 10 (top)	Kellogg Company, Battle Creek, Michigan
Photo p. 9 (below)	American Dairy Association
Photo p. 13	Taylor Wine Company

Dutch tiles photographed on page 84 with the permission of the Metropolitan Museum of Art, New York City.